D0652635

HOUSTON
BEER

★ HOUSTON BEER

A HEADY HISTORY OF BREWING IN THE BAYOU CITY

Ronnie Crocker

Charleston  London

THE
History
PRESS

Published by The History Press
Charleston, SC 29403
www.historypress.net

First published 2012

Manufactured in the United States

ISBN 978.1.60949.537.4

Library of Congress Cataloging-in-Publication Data

Crocker, Ronnie.
Houston beer : a heady history of brewing in the Bayou City / Ronnie Crocker.
p. cm.
Includes bibliographical references and index.
ISBN 978-1-60949-537-4
1. Beer industry--Texas--Houston--History. 2. Brewing industry--Texas--Houston--History.
3. Breweries--Texas--Houston--History. 4. Beer--Texas--Houston--History. 5. Brewers-
-Texas--Houston--Biography. 6. Houston (Tex.)--History. 7. Houston (Tex.)--Economic
conditions. 8. Houston (Tex.)--Biography. I. Title.
HD9397.U53H683 2012
338.4'766342097641411--dc23
2012006560

Contents

Acknowledgements

Long hours alone at the computer notwithstanding, writing a book is a joyfully collaborative effort, and I am grateful to every person you see quoted, cited in a photo caption or named as an interview subject in the bibliography of this book. Each contributed, either by taking the time to talk with me, sharing important documents and memorabilia or—like those nineteenth-century newspaper writers—leaving something behind that remains worth reading. Thank you, all.

Special thanks to Philip Brogniez, Susan Lieberman Seekatz and Ralph Stenzel, who answered the call of a stranger who said he was writing a book and wanted their help. I hope you enjoyed sharing your stories with me as much as I have enjoyed setting them down here.

Much appreciation to the following:

To Kyrie O'Connor of *Wait, Wait...Don't Tell Me!* fame. For three years, Kyrie was my editor at the *Houston Chronicle*, and she was an immediate and enthusiastic supporter of the Beer, TX blog I write for chron.com. She graciously read early chapters of this book and encouraged me to keep going.

To Burke Watson, my great friend and tenacious former *Chronicle* colleague, for putting his excellent editing skills to work on the draft.

To Joyce Lee, the indefatigable *Chronicle* librarian, for tracking down any number of old stories, books and photographs.

To the excellent *Chronicle* photographers whose work enlivens these pages, to Howard Decker for giving me permission to use their pictures and to Susan Barber and Ken Ellis for designing the Beer, TX logo.

ACKNOWLEDGEMENTS

To the Houston Public Library, the Metropolitan Research Center and librarians and archivists everywhere for curating such an immense volume of material for anyone who wants to see it, whenever the need arises. Please squawk loudly whenever your elected officials talk about cutting funding for this valuable work.

To *Mountain Brew* author Ed Sealover and The History Press commissioning editor Becky LeJeune for getting me into this project. I never cursed their names once.

To Patricia Shepherd, my partner in life, another thoughtful reader of drafts and a boon companion on many beer adventures past and future.

And to the countless readers, brewers and home-brewers, bartenders and bar owners, sales reps, distributors, beer geeks and otherwise enthusiastic participants in this great city's beer-loving community. They have made writing Beer, TX and this book a rewarding journalistic endeavor.

Cheers!
Ronnie Crocker
February 1, 2012

Chapter 1

An Industrial Revolution in Beer

In the muggy late summer of 1913, Houston Ice and Brewing Company was hardly alone in promoting its beer as the best in the city, even if it was the only one bold enough to boast that its flagship, a lager called Southern Select, constituted a "potent muscle-building liquid nutrient."

Frequent advertisements in the *Houston Chronicle* declared Blatz "the finest beer ever brewed" and Pabst the "finest for forty years." Old Fashioned Lager, alluding to the wilting Gulf Coast heat, offered to "cut your suffering in half" with "this best of summer beverages," while Budweiser crowed that it had sold 175 million bottles the year before. These national brands also were given to touting their "exclusive" local distributors, while the American Brewing Association, independently run at Railroad and 2nd Streets in Houston for twenty years by a certain Adolphus Busch of St. Louis, described its Pilsener as "pure as the sun's rays" and asked, "May we deliver you a case? Just phone Preston 73."

But then on Wednesday, September 3, Houston Ice and Brewing dropped a marketing bombshell on its competitors. A rare full-page ad, illustrated with woodcut drawings of genteel women and men riding horses across what could be the English countryside, urged Houstonians to "Follow the Call of Triumph!" Southern Select could now credibly be called "the world's finest bottled beer" after earning the Grand Prix of the Exposition medal at an international competition in Ghent, Belgium. The beer, brewed and bottled on the banks of the Buffalo Bayou at the four-block-wide Magnolia Brewery in Houston's industrial heart, had outranked 4,067 other beers by a jury of "the greatest European scientists, chemists and brewery experts." The

Follow the Call of Triumph!

You are invited to become a member of "the Jury of Awards"—'for Texas'—give a thorough trial to

SOUTHERN SELECT BOTTLED BEER

Made in Houston at the famous Magnolia Brewery by the Houston Ice & Brewing Company

Awarded the Grand Prix at the International Exposition at Ghent, Belgium, in Competition With the Product of 4068 Leading Breweries of the World

Every high class brewmaster covets the distinction of the scantest consideration and mention at the world famous Centennial Expositions of Belgium. The Jury of Awards—a board composed of the greatest European scientists, chemists and brewery experts—after careful deliberation and the most searching chemical tests honored Southern Select Bottled Beer with the Grand Prix of the International Exposition. No other American Beer gained this honor test of consideration.

Southern Select

The Grand Prize Winning Bottled Beer
—you will find it a beverage of delectable excellence as well as scientifically correct and ABSOLUTELY PURE.

All the World Loves a Winner

Be Your Own Judge—test the nutritive and flesh building qualities of Southern Select—there is no pleasanter tasting beer, none nearer perfect from any standpoint. You will agree with the International Grand Jury of Awards and Pronounce

Southern Select
"The World's Finest Bottled Beer"

Houston Ice & Brewing Company
Brewers and Bottlers of "Southern Select"   Houston, U. S. A.

The Beer That Has Made Houston Triumphant

Houston Ice and Brewing ran a series of full-page ads in the *Houston Chronicle* to commemorate the international accolades for its Southern Select. *Collection of Philip Brogniez.*

hometown brewers bought another full-page ad on Sunday, September 7, and two slightly smaller ones the following two Sundays to elaborate.

> *The beer that achieved this signal distinction was made in Houston last December; it was four months old when it was bottled and exported and had been four months in the bottles when the award was made. It was made, aged, handled and packed exactly as every bottle of Southern Select is made, aged and handled for consumption in the home, club and cafe.*

"The beer that has made Houston triumphant," the first ads declared, a poke at the already famous slogan for Schlitz. According to a later report, the jab was sharpened for a downtown celebration outside the Rice Hotel, when a banner was raised declaring Southern Select "The Beer that Made Milwaukee Jealous." The local press jumped on the bandwagon, proclaiming in a news story that "Texas jumps into the limelight" with a locally brewed beer that

Houston Ice and Brewing Company operated the Magnolia Brewery on the banks of the Buffalo Bayou from the 1890s until Prohibition. *Collection of Bart Truxillo.*

"put Milwaukee out of the running and leaves St. Louis nowhere." The writer quoted company vice-president Robert Autrey as crediting "the soil of Texas," the local water and the brewery's own standard operating procedures with contributing to a beer the brewers already considered "first rank."

The bragging was understandable. The men of Houston Ice and Brewing's Magnolia Brewery had brought international recognition to a city that was still in the early stages of its transformation from muddy frontier town to oil-rich metropolis.

But the glory faded quickly. Within a decade, Prohibition had wrecked the brewing industry and triggered the demise of the Magnolia; all that remains of the grand, turreted complex is the building that housed executive offices and a cafe where the city's power brokers discussed deals over suds and nickel sandwiches. Nearly a century of sharp growth, immigration and international commerce have smoothed away most of Houston's rough edges, and the city now is better known for its glittering skyscrapers, many of them built with energy wealth; for Mission Control, where a team of NASA engineers received man's first message from the moon; and for the sprawling

Texas Medical Center staffed by the world's finest warriors in the struggle against cancer, heart disease and other enemies of the flesh.

The six million people who call the metropolitan area home today are a diverse bunch, but their palates and sensibilities are very much aligned with urbanites across the country. They frequent farmer's markets, follow gourmet food trucks on Twitter and pay a premium for "locally sourced" meats and vegetables. Growing numbers, too, are showing a preference for craft beer over the mass-produced light, lower-calorie Bud, Miller and Coors products that have dominated the domestic industry for decades. At the beginning of 2008, there was a single craft brewery in Houston catering to these emerging tastes; four years later, there are five within an hour's drive of downtown and a handful of hopefuls in varying stages of development.

For the vast majority of people buying the ales, stouts and lagers made by these small, independently owned breweries, Houston's beer history dates back only a few years at most. Those of a certain generation, many of whom were first exposed to "good beer" through European travel or maybe a favorite college professor, can trace it back to October 14, 1978, the day President Jimmy Carter signed legislation that made home-brewing legal in post-Prohibition America, or to the mid-1990s, when an act of the Texas Legislature led to a short-lived boom in brewpub restaurants that made their own beer on site. For ancient history, Houstonians may look eastward, to the 136-acre Anheuser-Busch complex that opened in 1966 and pumps out 12.5 million barrels of Bud Light, ZiegenBock and other brands each year.

You can't blame all of this on the shortcomings of modern attention spans, for the record of local brewing's earliest history is frustratingly incomplete. Breweries were mentioned frequently in the press, but often with the barest of context. An expansion was noted, or the city's help was enlisted to build a brick wall, or a freak lightning strike was reported to have knocked over a boiler and scalded a worker nearly to death. In a one-paragraph mention, a Bridgeport, Connecticut firm seemed serious about building a brewery in Houston, but there was no follow-up. Similarly, in June 1894, a "Prof. Rheimstein" from Nuremburg was reportedly in the Houston Heights testing artesian water and telling people that a brewery was coming within the year to make Bavarian beer in the neighborhood.

One item in the *Galveston Daily News* "Town Notes" roundup on March 29, 1890, said, in its entirety: "An enterprising and practical business man has purchased half a block of ground at a convenient point for the purpose of erecting a brewery." A "Town Notes" follow-up in July noted the project "is being allowed a rest on account of the absence of several of the gentlemen interested in the same. The success of a brewery establishment is, however, well assured."

For the enterprises that actually opened, success was fleeting at best. As early as the late 1940s, a photo in a Houston newspaper showed the brick hulk of an abandoned factory —"the old American Brewing…a casualty of prohibition"—and pointed out that trees had taken root on the third floor, descended over the intervening thirty years from "sprigs, doubtless carried by birds." While individual brewers and breweries occasionally are referenced in local histories, they often appear as names on lists that, while painstakingly compiled, lie as flat on the page as birth and death dates hung from a genealogical tree. Even the *Encyclopedia of Texas Breweries: Pre-Prohibition 1836–1918* concludes that the early era "can best be described as a maze of speculation, rumor and forgotten history."

But drawing some conclusions from this record, sparse as it may be, brings to life some of the forbears of today's craft-beer pioneers. Houston, it turns out, has known booms not just in lumber, cotton, oil and exploration of the heavens but in the ancient art of brewing as well. Besides those brash early oil drillers known as wildcatters, the city boasted wildcatters of ale, with outsized personalities of their own. As the nineteenth century wound down, it was possible for visitors to board a train at the Grand Central depot and pass two "handsome and large" breweries, Houston Ice and Brewing to one side and American Brewing on the other, each with brick smokestacks protruding from multistory factory buildings. By then, beer had become big business, and like the robber barons of rail and steel, the beer bosses soon would attract the attention of regulators. In 1915, these two Houston breweries were among seven in Texas sanctioned by the state attorney general for collusion, price fixing and interfering in the political process to influence liquor laws. It was, the government said, a pattern of behavior that existed "long prior to the year 1901."

A generation later, after the failed national experiment with Prohibition had shuttered these early giants, no less a colorful character than Howard Hughes would become part of the beer timeline, owning a successful brewery east of downtown for thirty years. Actually making the beer were brewmasters like Frantz Brogniez, whose Southern Select recipe won that Grand Prix in 1913, and Charles Lieberman, who garnered other international medals in the 1950s while at Hughes's Gulf Brewing Company. These were not factory hacks but real Renaissance characters. Brogniez, a Belgian immigrant whose interests ranged from the violin to the emerging science of biology, had studied under Louis Pasteur, hobnobbed with Henry Ford and penned several compositions of classical music. Lieberman, descended from a brewing family in Pennsylvania, wrote poetry in his spare time, and after Gulf Brewing closed in 1963, he joined the history-making team at NASA as a safety engineer.

They, in turn, were part of a deeper local tradition. In fact, a century before Americans ever heard the term "craft beer," men like Peter Gabel were practicing this very craft in Houston. A hand-drawn map of Houston from 1873 shows two brewery sites on the orderly street grid of downtown.

The earliest Anglo settlers in Texas are said to have fermented persimmons for beer, crushed apples for cider and made wine from native grapes. But in rapidly industrializing Houston, brewing quickly became an industrial affair. By 1912, not long after Brogniez arrived from Terre Haute, Indiana, with three kids and an ailing wife in search of a warmer climate, the American and Magnolia breweries employed some five hundred workers at union wages of two to five dollars a day—higher than in sawmills, cotton mills, packinghouses and railroad yards—to staff three eight-hour shifts each day. Their working conditions were described at the time as "exceptionally good."

So even as the pro-Prohibition "drys" built momentum in Texas, as elsewhere across the country—those Old Fashioned Lager ads assured customers of discreet deliveries, "in plain boxes on unlettered wagons"—drinking was a ubiquitous fact of community life, as it had been from the beginning.

It wasn't spilled liquor that muddied the streets of early Houston, though a visitor could be forgiven for thinking so. One of the first settlers, arriving by boat in early January 1837, recalled having to search the banks of Buffalo Bayou for "stakes and footprints" that marked the frontier outpost, then home to barely a dozen souls. Once he found the markers, he described his initial impression of Houston this way: "A few tents were located not far away; one large one was used as a saloon."

By 1838, a deputy constable could count forty-seven establishments selling alcoholic drinks in a city of probably fewer than two thousand residents; the first church wasn't built until two years later. Despite the city's first

A Heady History of Brewing in the Bayou City

Abstinence Society meeting in February 1839 and what has been described as a "wave of temperance" activity three years later, Houstonians never lost their thirst for strong drink. Houston's mayor in 1854 expressed his thanks to members of the Turnverein, a German social group that promoted "athletics and intellectual pursuits" for immigrants, for their help in fighting a fire by gifting them with "two dozen bottles of ale and porter, which you will please accept as a small token of my appreciation." During the 1890s, it was said, "the saloons never closed." Even after the discovery of oil began to remake Houston into an international center of commerce, a history book described a place with "beer parlors in abundance and an equal abundance of church spires."

Perhaps this should come as no surprise for a city that wasn't founded so much as willed into an improbable existence. When brothers Augustus C. and John K. Allen, land speculators and native New Yorkers, bought what would become the original town site in August 1836, barely four months had passed since revolutionist Texans had wrested a bloody independence from the Mexican army a few miles away at San Jacinto. The Allen brothers promoted their city as a potential thriving port, though it lay fifty miles inland on swampy flatlands that were prone to epidemics of yellow fever. They also saw it as the perfect seat of the new national government and named it for the hero of San Jacinto, Sam Houston, who also happened to be the first Republic of Texas president.

The Allens' lobbying was successful, if only briefly. The legislators arrived in 1837, began discussing a move almost immediately and bolted for Austin in 1839.

Despite this setback, the city grew rapidly. It soon had two sawmills, a brick factory and even a luxury hotel. The railroads and, yes, shipping helped the city prosper in both the timber and cotton trades. From the beginning, Houston offered huge rewards to men—white men, it must be acknowledged, in that shameful era of legal slavery—with big dreams and a strong work ethic.

And it offered plenty of places for these men to blow off steam.

"The main businesses in the beginning were mercantile," says local historian Betty Chapman. "That and saloons…Houston had the reputation of being wild and woolly."

Onto this "wild and woolly" scene in 1844 marched a Bavarian native in his early thirties, "the possessor of a rugged constitution, strong arms and energy," who would be one of the first to profit from turning Houston water into beer. Peter Gabel is credited with founding the city's first commercial brewery, perhaps as early as 1849, with another immigrant, Henry Schulte. Although details of the Gabel Brewery are scarce, production certainly was small in scale. As the *Encyclopedia of Texas Breweries* notes: "The 1860 census listed eleven breweries throughout the State of Texas. Houston had three breweries that produced an estimated total of 4,300 barrels of beer annually, and two of the three were powered by steam engines."

Peter Gabel, a German immigrant and one of Houston's earliest brewers, sponsored this float during the 1870 Volksfest parade downtown. *Photo courtesy of the Houston Metropolitan Research Center, Houston Public Library. (Mss 0157-1205).*

A Heady History of Brewing in the Bayou City

Both Gabel and Schulte became wealthy businessmen, and each left a strong impression on his adopted city. The Houston Turnverein, in fact, was founded in Gabel's home, with him as one of the original members. An 1870 photograph from the club's annual Volksfest celebration shows a float sponsored by P. Gabel decorated with grapevines and carrying what looks to be a wine barrel along the parade route. Inscribed on the side of the wagon, in German, is the old adage "in vino veritas," meaning in wine there is truth.

Gabel had come to the United States in 1840, living for a time in Cincinnati and then St. Louis, and his arrival in Houston coincided with the beginning of a decade of heavy German immigration that would have a lasting influence on the city and its culture. Not only did these newcomers establish social organizations such as the Turnverein, but they also clamored for lager beer, which was more familiar and more to their liking than the English-style ales usually served.

Gabel's was the embodiment of the immigration success story. Born in Herxheim am Berg, Rhine Phalz, Bavaria, in 1813, he trained as a cooper, and his work in Houston included cutting wood, coopering and starting a soap factory. The latter enterprise failed, but the brewery prevailed, and he made beer at least until the start of the Civil War, when breweries ostensibly were illegal in the Confederacy. According to his 1896 obituary in the *Houston Daily Post*, Gabel had then found opportunity in other intoxicants:

> *During the war he started a distillery and made a prime article of whisky, and in the days that tried men's souls $1500 a gallon was a fancy price paid for liquor from his still, but it is claimed that the thirsty often exchanged that sum in Confederate money for a gallon of the juice of the corn. He also made cider from dried apples and then started a wine business. For years and years he was noted as being the owner of the finest wine cellar in the Southwest. The large vaults in his buildings are filled with wine in casks and bottles from floor to roof. He was a connoisseur in Rhine wine and dealt exclusively in that brand.*

During the 1870s, Gabel also could claim a direct connection to at least two of the three breweries that were then operating in Houston, through his half brother, John Wagner, and his business partner, Henry Schulte. The exhaustively researched *American Breweries II* lists these Houston businesses as Wagner and Herman (1874–79), G. Schulte (1874–75) and Fritz Hahn (1874–75), though it doesn't provide further detail. Wagner's 1891 obituary sheds a tad more light, even if it doesn't jibe perfectly in some details. The obit says Wagner, "one of the good citizens of Houston," worked at the

Gabel brewery from his arrival in Houston in 1850 until 1869 and that he and Charles Hermann took over as partners in 1879.

A more recent account, from local historian Louis Aulbach's hefty *Buffalo Bayou: An Echo of Houston's Wilderness Beginnings*, describes another local brewery operated by another German immigrant family, the Floecks. "Each of these breweries were family owned craft breweries and probably produced modest quantities of beer in season," Aulbach writes.

What this record makes clear is that the city's earliest German immigrants brought a lively part of their native culture with them and founded a tradition in Houston that endures today.

The *Daily Post* hailed Gabel upon his death as "one of the landmarks," and it concluded that "his busy life was closely identified with the growth and progress of Houston from a struggling hamlet to an imperial city." He was recalled in a Galveston newspaper as "one of a very few octogenarians

Gabel died a wealthy gentleman and is buried at Glenwood Cemetery. His grave site is not far from that of Howard Hughes. *Photo by Ronnie Crocker.*

in the city of Houston," and he was said to be comforted in his final days by a daughter and son-in-law. He died with what would be a millionaire's fortune today, the owner of several properties in addition to his home at 313 San Jacinto, with a total estate formally estimated at $50,000. As further evidence of his position in Houston society, one of the executors of his will was James A. Baker, an attorney with the city's oldest law firm and the grandfather of a future U.S. secretary of state, and he was buried in the city's exclusive Glenwood Cemetery.

A tall obelisk marks his grave beneath the towering oak trees that shade this elegant resting place, where Gabel shares real estate with such Houston notables as Hughes, the eccentric tycoon who was known as the world's richest man, and Anson Jones, the last president of the Republic of Texas, who fatally shot himself in a downtown hotel in 1858.

Like Gabel, Henry Schulte, too, was fondly remembered by his contemporaries. According to his own obituary in the *Galveston Daily News*, Schulte's 1877 death of apoplexy while in Frankfurt, Germany, where he'd recently returned with his family after retiring from the grocery business in Galveston, "was entirely unexpected, and will surprise and pain his numerous friends." He was known for his "strict integrity" and "fine business qualities," the paper reported, pointing out that a second Houston brewery co-founded by Schulte was "still in successful operation under management of his brother."

By the time of Gabel's death nineteen years later, all these early breweries were gone, and the only physical reminder of the beer Gabel had made was a sign that hung over a bar on Preston Avenue, not far from his home on San Jacinto. Advances in refrigeration and transportation had given Houstonians access to products from the powerful burghers of brew based in St. Louis and Milwaukee.

But brewing wasn't dead in Houston. Rather, it was undergoing an Industrial Revolution of its own.

In March 1893, the American Brewing Association bragged that it was building "the largest brewery in Texas," right here in Houston, with the capacity to produce 100,000 barrels of beer annually and 250 tons of ice daily in a sprawling plant that featured four smokestacks. American commenced operations in the fall, under the ownership of Adolphus Busch, with a reported $350,000 in capital, and it began delivering beer the following spring. Busch explained on January 1:

> *Although our new brewery, which is the largest in Texas and one of the model breweries of the country, has been completed and in operation since over two months, we will not be ready to put our own beer on the market before March 1—so it will have sufficient age and "lager"—but we can assure you that it will be equal in purity and flavor to the best brands of St. Louis or Milwaukee and superior to any made in the South.*

A collectible plate from the American Brewing Association brewery that Adolphus Busch built in Houston in the 1890s. *Collection of Ralph W. Stenzel Jr. Photographed by Ronnie Crocker.*

Busch by this time was head of St. Louis–based Anheuser-Busch and was in the process of making it the nation's most powerful beer company. Although his American Brewery was not formally part of Anheuser-Busch, it took over all local distribution of Anheuser-Busch products and pledged "that we shall in the future continue to furnish the trade in this city and vicinity with all their famous brands of beer, especially the celebrated Faust and Budweiser."

It offered something for "farmers and dairymen," too: beginning in December, the brewery would have spent grain for sale.

Competition came from Houston Ice and Brewing, which was incorporated in April 1892 by local owners who had raised $250,000 in capital. They began production the following year in what they called the Magnolia Brewery, which featured forty-two fermentation tanks of 85 barrels each and a pair of ice machines that could crank out 225 tons of ice daily. Construction was estimated to have cost $200,000 (nearly $5 million in today's dollars), and the original capacity was listed at 110,000 barrels annually.

That April, the brewery opened its doors and invited the public to tour the facility and sample the wares. An illustration accompanying an invitation published in the *Galveston Daily News* shows a grand complex, five stories high in places, with multiple turrets and a pair of belching smokestacks. Though the brewery owners describe their "pride and pleasure" in doing so, they also allude to the growing prohibitionist sentiment that portended the disaster that would befall them less than three decades later: "We therefore call on all good citizens, even those who are not friendly to our cause, to throw aside their little personal prejudices and give us the pleasure of their presence at the opening and partake with us of the product of the farm after it having passed through the skillful manipulations of a scientific artist and made useful and beneficial for the use of man, woman and child."

There was no boycott, and Carry Nation didn't crash the party, hatchet in hand. In fact, the open house drew more than ten thousand visitors "to quaff the amber liquid and blow off the foam," a newspaper correspondent said, adding that the beer "was freer than water because nobody took the latter. Before noon the thirsty friends of the firm had consumed 120 kegs of beer."

The party was far from over: "At that hour an armistice was declared and hostilities were suspended until 5 o'clock, when they were resumed with greater earnestness than before, and the onslaught lasted until 10 o'clock this evening…A half dozen kegs of beer were on tap at one time. Nobody thirsted and nobody rested."

Workers in the Magnolia Brewery's barrelhouse keg Houston beer in this undated photograph. *Collection of Bart Truxillo.*

The celebration, which involved "many of the best citizens of the town," kicked off a fast beginning for Houston Ice and Brewing. Less than a year after opening, the company began running ads for a sixteen-foot by sixty-inch boiler "for sale cheap" because the Magnolia Brewery had already outgrown it. The equipment had to be removed, the owners explained, "on account of being too small for our purpose."

In 1898, the brewery president, Hugh Hamilton, was working on a deal to ship "a large consignment of bottled beer" to Havana, a business deal that was hailed for demonstrating "what the possibilities are for developing a good trade after the settlement of the war difficulties." Eight years later, Houston Ice and Brewing would indeed launch its first ship bound for Key West, Florida, with a load of kegs that would then make their way to the island of Cuba.

Both the Magnolia and American breweries were sizable operations, especially by the standards of today's U.S. microbreweries. A water commissioner's report published around the time of their opening found that, with a total of five wells, the two plants accounted for nearly 20 percent of the 5.2 million gallons of well water generated daily for the entire city of Houston. Along with three ice works, a bottling works and a "sodawater bottling plant," the breweries were listed among the "principal railways, manufactories and industries, etc. of the city" in a year-end accounting on December 17, 1893, by the *Houston Daily Post* headlined, "BUSIER THAN EVER is the good city of Houston and its people." The same article made note of the city's half-dozen cotton compresses "claiming to be the largest in the world," four large cottonseed oil mills, 164 arc lights and more than fifty miles of electric car lines.

By 1913, the Magnolia complex alone covered four city blocks and had increased its capacity to 175,000 barrels through a series of additions that included building a span over Buffalo Bayou. It was producing Southern Select, Richelieu and "the standard keg product." The company stock by then was valued at $300,000—"not one dollar of which," a published report noted proudly, "is owned outside of Texas."

These heady times wouldn't last forever, and relatively few people outside an ardent core of history buffs or memorabilia collectors have likely even heard of these once-mighty engines of brew.

But, man, what a ride it was while it lasted.

Chapter 2

The Other Boom at the Turn of the Century

A great poet, John Reymershoffer wasn't.
But the president of the Galveston Brewing Company nevertheless left behind a little insight into a growing conflict of his day when he penned these words for the island brewery's grand opening on February 3, 1897:

Wine is good for some occasion,
Whisky leads a man astray,
Champagne is the rich man's ration,
Beer's the drink of every day.

Beer's the beverage of the nation
For old and young, child, man and wife;
The progress of civilization,
It's next to bread—the staff of life.

Beer is for the people, tonic;
Gives them health or strengthens it,
But it will not suit the chronic
Teetotaler or hypocrite.

Give me lager in the morning,
Give me lager after noon,
When the midday sun is burning,
When at midnight shines the moon.

A Heady History of Brewing in the Bayou City

Give me lager on a Sunday
When social time I can afford,
Give me lager on a feast day
And I'll truly praise the Lord.

But let the lager be refreshing,
Foaming, sparkling, cool and clear,
Malt and hops of purest mashing—
Let it be "Galveston Beer."

Certainly, Reymershoffer, addressing the crowd at midafternoon as a sheet imprinted with his poem was unrolled with a flourish behind him, hadn't overstated Galvestonians' enthusiasm for beer, particularly one that was light enough to refresh in the subtropical heat; in 1894 alone, the city's residents had consumed more than forty thousand barrels of the stuff. Indeed, the plant just fifty miles south of Houston would remain in operation, under various owners, making "Galveston beer" off and on for most of the next ninety years.

And, too, the business community was thrilled by the prospects for the plant with an initial 50,000-barrel capacity, expandable to 100,000 barrels, that was launched with $400,000 in capital investment. St. Louis beer barons Adolphus

A postcard for High Grade beer shows the original Galveston Brewery, built in partnership by local investors and St. Louis beer barons Adolphus Busch and William Lemp. *Collection of Ralph W. Stenzel Jr.*

Busch and William J. Lemp had put up half that amount, but the rest came from local investors. The hometown newspaper had written effusively about Busch's plans, which included shipping beer to other Gulf ports and even the West Indies on refrigerated vessels, and it calculated how much money the brewery and ice plant would keep on the island, since most of what was being spent on beer at the time was going to seven out-of-town beer companies and the city was importing an estimated twenty to thirty tons of ice daily.

The brick, Romanesque-style factory must have been an impressive sight for those taking that first public tour, with a five-story brew house and elevator to bring malt from the storeroom to the various floors; a "refrigerating room" with a pair of one-hundred-ton machines and one fifty-ton machine; and a two-story boiler room hosting three 250-horsepower, coal-fired boilers. The Santa Fe Railway laid a new track on the north side, and a local line put in a switch to the west, establishing a link to the growing, and about to boom, Beaumont area. Not surprisingly, given the lack of environmental concerns or regulation at the time, a twelve-inch drain for runoff ran for 1,500 feet directly to Galveston Bay.

The *Galveston Daily News* praised the factory as "a model in point of design and convenience" and described the stockhouse this way:

> *This building is four stories in height and filled with the big vats in which the finished product remains for two or three months after having come from the brewhouse. In the rear of this is the racking house, where the beer is filled off from the big storage tanks for shipment. On the south end of both these buildings is the wash house, where the returned kegs are washed and inspected and later sent to the racking house to be filled. Besides these buildings are wagon sheds and outhouses.*

Workers had broken ground on the complex in September 1895, and the ice plant was turning out "the crystal product" by the following July. The first batch of beer was brewed that October. "Thus," reported the *Daily News*, "the beer drank yesterday is four months old, which is considered the proper age for good drinking beer."

Galveston prided itself on being a worldly city, and the flags on display that day represented countries from Mexico and Cuba to India, from Germany and France to Turkey, "almost every flag under the sun." The celebration was attended by a Mexican consul, as well as executives from breweries in Houston, San Antonio and Fort Worth.

Yet Reymershoffer betrayed the undercurrent of unease among those in the booze business as the century drew to its close. The executive/poet's swipe at the "chronic teetotaler or hypocrite" alluded to the growing clamor to outlaw liquor altogether. A year and a half earlier, the Texas president of the Woman's Christian Temperance Union, Helen M. Stoddard, had singled out her state and Busch in particular in a fiery speech to a prohibitionist crowd in New York:

> *Texas has a very good local option law, and through it we may be a prohibition state before very long. Of course national prohibition is what we must have, and local option is a good way to educate sentiment in that direction. Adolphus Busch feels so worried over the way Texas is doing that he wrote us a letter of advice, in which he threatened to withdraw all his millions from Texas if we didn't cease being so fanatical. If prohibition does not prohibit, why this threat? Sam Jones says, "The hit dog howls," and I am glad we have hit the brewers.*

Reymershoffer's was a passing jab, easily laughed off during the sudsy celebration. The failed national experiment with Prohibition was still more than two decades away. For now, Galveston had a new beer plant run by a superintendent descended from a family of brewers in Munich, who soon would be producing beers like those brewed in that famed German city. On this chilly afternoon, the mood on the corner of Postoffice and 34th Streets, not far from downtown, was ebullient. "A flow of compliments accompanies the flow of beer," a correspondent wrote of the grand opening, adding, "Sweet music was discoursed and to its inspiring influences the masses drank beer."

The Houston-Galveston region now had three major breweries in full swing. Not even a catastrophic hurricane three and a half years later could put them out of business.

Galveston-brewed High Grade Beer was promoted as "liquid food." *Collection of Ralph W. Stenzel Jr.*

The 1890s proved consequential for the local beer scene in ways large and small. The American, Magnolia and Galveston breweries were founded during the decade, but so was the Anti-Saloon League, a prohibitionist lobby whose side would prevail in the coming battle over booze. Busch's American Brewery joined a revolution in drinking convenience by replacing corks in its bottled beers with crown bottle caps, which the brewery hailed as "the latest and best invention of the age." An illustrated advertisement showed how much easier it now was to pop a top on a cold one with a little girl exclaiming, "I can open it, mama." Pint bottles of Dixie Pale and Hackerbrau dark were going for $1.05 per dozen; quart bottles ran $1.60 for twelve.

Meanwhile, five thousand miles away in Belgium, another unfolding drama would have a lasting impact here as well: Frantz Brogniez's marriage was falling apart.

The man who would become Houston's most celebrated brewer, Frantz Hector Brogniez, was born into a well-to-do Belgian family—one grandmother was a countess—in 1860 at an estate in Haine-Saint-Paul,

Belgium-born Frantz Brogniez became the most celebrated of Houston's pre-Prohibition brewers. *Collection of Philip Brogniez.*

less than twenty miles from the French border. His privileged station meant travel at an early age to such countries as Austria, Germany and Russia and the opportunity to study music with some of the era's most accomplished teachers. His interest in playing the violin and composing orchestral works was lifelong. According to a family history compiled by his grandson, Brogniez, while a student at the University of Louvain, was president of the school's symphony and played in a string double quartet; he once performed for Kaiser Wilhelm and was presented a medal by King Leopold II for one of his compositions.

"It has been said," Philip Brogniez wrote of his grandfather, "that at the age of nineteen, while in Paris and attending a performance of the famous Concert Cologne, the conductor had taken ill, whereupon Frantz volunteered to continue the program and did so, conducting without prior preparation."

Yet it was no surprise that, upon his 1882 graduation, with honors, he would go to work in a small brewery in Lichtervelde and establish a brewing school there two years later. His family had been making beer since 1752, and the scientific aspect of the trade appealed to another of Brogniez's passions, the emerging field of bacteriology. Louis Pasteur had published his *Studies on Fermentation* just six years earlier, and Brogniez learned personally from this master.

"He was a guy who was very talented in many different areas," Philip Brogniez says of his grandfather. "He was a microbiologist—at the turn of the century that was a big deal. He was a biochemist, by the standards back then."

By 1895, this musically inclined scientist, fluent in several languages, French, Flemish and English among them, had landed in Brussels and was running his own brewery. But his destiny was not to be a European gentleman. Just a year later, he was on a ship bound for New York's Ellis Island with a woman who wasn't his wife, the first leg in a sixteen-year odyssey that would bring him to Houston.

Brogniez was still in college when he married Cornelie van der Hulst. They had three children, one of whom, a boy, died at an early age. For reasons the young brewer's United States–born descendants never learned, Cornelie moved to France and took their two daughters with her. Did she simply desert her husband? Or had he callously abandoned his family and she left the country in search of a fresh start? The loss of a child can be devastating for a couple, and a split under that kind of stress would not be unprecedented. Whatever had transpired, when Brogniez arrived in New York aboard the steamship *Adriatic*, he was in the company of Alida Grymonprez, a woman he'd met and fallen in love with in Lichtervelde.

The couple settled in Detroit, where because of the circumstances of their relationship, they were denied marriage by the Catholic Church and were forced to slip across the border to take care of that detail in Canada.

"I'm guessing he left partly for the opportunities in the United States and partly because of family troubles," Philip Brogniez says, filling in the blanks for a grandfather he never met. "He goes to Detroit. What he knows, mostly, is how to brew beer."

Just a few months after his arrival there, Brogniez started a Belgian-style brewery on Mack Avenue that became Tivoli—whose motto was "Say it backwards: I love it!"—though Philip Brogniez says the name change was forced upon his grandfather by investors who took control of the business while Brogniez was on a trip to Belgium attending to his dying father. Nonetheless, he remained with the company and is prominently featured in the 1903 book *100 Years of Brewing: A Complete History of the Brewing Industry of the World*. Accompanied by a half-page portrait, the Tivoli entry extols Brogniez's brewing skills and notes that he began construction on the facility there in November 1896 and that under the Tivoli ownership the brewery

A page from Brogniez's beer-recipe book, handwritten in French. *Collection of Philip Brogniez. Photographed by Ronnie Crocker.*

grew rapidly, to an annual capacity of "seventy-five thousand barrels of lager beer."

But Brogniez's travels were far from over. In 1903, tragedy struck the household, when Alida succumbed to tuberculosis. In a moving final letter to her husband, she asked that he marry her sister, Alice, so their children would be raised by a relative. Brogniez honored Alida's wish the following year after her parents brought Alice over from Belgium to start a new life as a seventeen-year-old stepmom to her niece and nephew. The new family left Detroit shortly afterward and moved to Terre Haute, Indiana, where Brogniez had been hired to run what became the Peoples Brewery. As superintendent, he helped design the brewery's impressive, fortress-like brick factory with requisite smokestack and forty-thousand-barrel capacity. As brewmaster, he started the first batch on May 18, 1905.

Circumstances would change yet again a few years later, and this time they would bring Brogniez to Texas.

Houstonians' signature character trait, a wildly diverse brand of cosmopolitanism that is rich and international and not quite completely tamed, revealed itself early. The writer Lee Cohen Harby noted this in 1890. Her *Harper's* magazine essay "Texan Types and Contrasts" describes a Saturday market teeming with "vendors alone representing every nationality, Americans being far in the minority." She described German farmers and their "slow ox teams" hauling produce in from west of town, a pig-tailed Chinese man hawking "wonderful fans and cushions, brushes, teapots, Chinese lilies and what not" and a "thin-faced Italian [with] a wagon laden with game, all killed close by."

Even more striking are Harby's impressions of the crowd that gathered on the promenade:

> *The dude is in force, and the "masher" is not wanting; the men who stare and the girls who love to be stared at; sober matrons on house-keeping thoughts intent; flirtatious maidens who push through the crowd, and seem to have no idea that their manners are not of the best; natty negro wenches,*

pert of tongue and loose of demeanor; respectable colored "maumas," ample of girth, in spotless white aprons; strapping negro men and saucy bootblacks; merchants, lawyers and physicians; servant-girls and cooks; the haute-volée and the demimonde, and both in their best attire; policemen and tramps; old women, men on crutches, and babies in arms; black, white, brown and yellow—negroes, Americans, Mongolians, Irish, Dutch, French, Germans, Italians and Spanish—they are all there, laughing, talking, quarrelling, gesticulating, bargaining, gossiping, staring, keeping appointments and making new ones, being proper or improper, polite or rude, as the case may be. And this goes on from four to nine in winter, from five to ten in summer. Every Saturday evening it is re-enacted; the people never tire, it seems, but congregate weekly, year in and year out, in an endless repetition of the same thing. It is a wonderful scene, a bustling, moving picture of contrast and characters, and helps the traveller to better understand the prosperity of the State, which attracts one, and its rudenesses, which repel.

This "bustling, moving picture of contrast and characters" was in fact a hardworking bunch that fueled Houston's impressive growth throughout the late nineteenth century. However, the boom really began in the 1900s. At its onset, Houston's population was recorded as being just under forty-five thousand, and bank deposits averaged $118 per person, compared with $117 nationally. By the end of the decade, there were nearly seventy-nine thousand residents with an impressive $370 in per-capita bank deposits, nearly double the national average. Some of that growth and prosperity could be attributed to the lucky breaks of geology, but it took vision and effort to turn those breaks into something tangible and profitable.

In early 1900, Houston Ice and Brewing invested $180,000 in Magnolia expansions, including installation of a two-hundred-ton-capacity ice machine and construction of new buildings. "The present one-story building at the northern side of the brewery will be added to by putting two stories of brick above it," the *Daily Post* reported. "This addition will be a valuable one to the brewery, will add to its room and will be put up at some expense. In addition to this another building will be put up on the banks of the bayou to accommodate other machinery to be ordered. Several boilers additional will be needed and a new engine for the ice plant."

Meanwhile, two events that would have seemed inconceivable at the time were about to profoundly reshape all of Southeast Texas, but especially Houston. On September 8, the "great Galveston hurricane" roared ashore with winds estimated at 145 miles per hour, swamping and destroying much of the island and killing between six thousand and twelve thousand people. In Houston, the storm killed a single person but damaged property, including the American Brewery. (The Galveston Brewery, however, was largely unscathed, and by September 12, it was actively involved in the disaster response, distributing ice "to all who would call.") For Houston, the storm would mean a surge of refugees fleeing the devastation and, over time, a permanent boost in economic advantage. Galvestonians got to work on a mind-boggling project to physically raise their elevation and install a miles-long concrete barrier to storm surge known as the Galveston Seawall. Their brewery kept making beer, including High Grade "liquid food" and the appreciatively named Seawall Bond.

The other transformative event occurred January 10, 1901, when the Gladys City Company struck oil at Spindletop, near Beaumont, and set Houston on its course to becoming a major energy center. That hefty rise in the bank-deposit numbers was no doubt inflated with newly acquired oil money. By April, the gusher had already made an impact on the beer business. The Magnolia became the second major manufacturer in the city to switch to oil to power its plant. Brewery president Hugh Hamilton told the *Daily Post* that he expected to save a substantial amount by hauling in 100 to 125 barrels a day from "the well at Beaumont" to keep three boilers fired up for a combined one thousand horsepower.

It wouldn't be the last time beer and oil would mix.

Chapter 3

Bad Behavior and
a Doomed National Experiment

Houstonians who see their city locked in a rivalry with Dallas may be disappointed to learn that the two most notable artifacts of Houston's distant beer history reside in a prosperous Big D suburb. There, in the downstairs den of his comfortable home, Philip Brogniez pays tribute to his grandfather with a framed "*diplome de grand prix*" and the accompanying first-place medal that Frantz Brogniez's Southern Select lager was awarded during an international competition for brewers in Ghent, Belgium. The design of the award is striking, a crowned and robed queen with hands extended to greet the three Roman muses as a farmer and barefoot girl approach her from behind. The imagery seems appropriate for beer, an agricultural product that seems to owe as much to artistic inspiration as it does to science.

Yet Brogniez, fifty-two at the time the award was made in August 1913 and a veteran brewmaster descended from a century-plus-long line of Belgian brewers, a man who appeared in newspaper ads photographed at his laboratory bench, gave full credit to the technical side of the craft.

"Our beer is brewed to pass the most rigid tests and inspections," he told a Houston newspaper writer. "I knew we had the finest grain and hops and water and now we have the highest certificate that our beer is chemically pure and scientifically perfect."

That it was made in Houston owed more to chance, specifically the perpetually shifting circumstances of Brogniez's personal life. In 1909, he

One of Frantz Brogniez's first brews after his arrival in Houston, a Southern Select lager he made at the Houston Ice and Brewing Company's Magnolia Brewery, earned him this medal in 1913. It's the Grand Prix of the International Exhibition in Ghent, Belgium. *Collection of Philip Brogniez.*

started looking to move because his young wife, Alice, twenty-six years her husband's junior, was ill, and a doctor advised the family to find a warmer climate.

Between his time brewing at Tivoli, in Detroit, and then as the designer and brewmaster of the successful Peoples Brewery in Terre Haute, Brogniez had earned a fine reputation among his peers nationally. In a personal letter accompanying his complimentary copy of *100 Years of Brewing*, the secretary-treasurer of the Pfaudler Company, which specialized in the F.F. vacuum system, praises Brogniez as "one of our most valued friends, and the one we recognize as the most skillful F.F. Brewers [*sic*] we have ever known." Philip Brogniez has the letter, dated April 20, 1903, which concludes, "It is a great pleasure to us to be the means of placing this picture and the little account of you where your children's children may see what sort of grandfather they had."

Pfaudler was based in Rochester, New York, but Brogniez's professional relationships extended southward as well. That included balmy Houston, just fifty miles from the Gulf of Mexico.

In 1912, Houston Ice and Brewing Company hired Brogniez as superintendent of its Magnolia Brewery. He and Alice moved down in March with their three children, the oldest two from his first wife, Alice's late sister, and they immediately embraced their new hometown. Just a year after their arrival, Brogniez was listed in a local who's who compiled by the Houston Press Club as "a Mason, an Elk, member of the Eagles, the German Club and the Young Business Men's Club." That same year, 1913, he helped Ima Hogg establish the Houston Symphony, suggesting that the city's elite class had embraced him as well. He moved easily in their circles, an intellectual from the Old World, the son of a prominent and politically active father who had been a longtime member of Belgium's Senate and an adviser to Kings Leopold II and Albert.

Brogniez arrived to find an expansive and still growing brewery complex. As his youngest son, the late architect Raymond Brogniez, recalled some years ago:

> The structures housing the business were of cut stone and reddish-brown brick. Erected in a style characteristic of breweries of the time, the cut stone first floor gave a substantial base for the four upper stories of the main building. The large main building covered nearly the entire block, with the stables and wagon building located across the street.
>
> The brew house, the heart of the brewing operation, occupied the front right portion of the buildings. The huge kettles, filtering process, and transfer piping required a building height of at least four stories. The fermenting cellars and storage vats were placed underground with the ice plant refrigeration equipment. The bottling shop was located in a two-story building to the left of the stables. Bottled and kegged beer was stored in a large building close to the railroad tracks—the Southern Pacific Depot was in the next block. The ice plant manufactured one hundred tons of ice per day and the brewery produced sixty thousand barrels of beer each year.

Brogniez recounted years later that he made Southern Select from a family recipe, one that was never written but rather passed down from father to son since the eighteenth century. In addition, Houston Ice and Brewing also made Richelieu, a dark Belgian-style beer named for the dark cardinal in *The Three Musketeers*, and Hiawatha, a so-called "near beer" that was advertised as "absolutely non-intoxicating." There was Magnolia Pale as well, and the magnolia flower was a featured motif on both beer bottles and in the glass windows of the brewery. When Brogniez took over its operations, the Magnolia Brewery was hailed as "the largest in the South." It had the capacity to make 175,000 barrels of beer a year, a production level that would rank it among the ten largest U.S. craft breweries today. It and the Busch-owned American Brewery were 2 of 347 factories in Houston that were manufacturing a combined $50 million in goods.

As Alice Brogniez stayed home and tended to the children's education and well-being, her husband brewed his masterpiece—even if he didn't realize it at the time. According to a family history, the brewer learned of the Exposition Universelie de Belgique belatedly:

> *The Exposition was held every couple of years and was a competition where beer from all over the world was put through a battery of tests. There was no time for any special beer to be brewed so Frantz had some beer pulled from the production line and had it sent with a friend that was traveling to Belgium. This particular year 4,096 beers were entered. Out of all these beers, Southern Select was the last one standing with three tests still to go. It was competing against itself. It won the Grand Prix.*

(Note: The number of entrants is variously listed among several accounts, but the newspaper ads that appeared immediately after the award was announced put the number at 4,067.)

In his own fairly low-key statement regarding the prize, Houston Ice and Brewing's vice-president, Robert Autrey, said it was a matter of pride that the entries had been plucked from a routine production run, telling the newspaper:

> *We are, of course, greatly pleased. But I may say that we were rather confident when the exhibit was entered. We had demonstrated to our own satisfaction that the products of the soil of Texas contained in a higher degree than may be found elsewhere those elements of excellence needful to the production of the finest beer. These combined with water containing the chemical elements necessary, and brewed under conditions which resulted in a chemically pure beer, assured us that we had attained to the first rank. The award of the Grande Prix certifies to the general excellence of the beer as well as to the fact that it is chemically pure. It must have been found to contain the necessary elements of nutriment and palatability as well. The*

Southern Select was brewed at the Magnolia Brewery until Prohibition. Afterward, the rights went to the Galveston-Houston Breweries. *Collection of Philip Brogniez.*

exhibit was taken at random from the product of the brewery and was merely a sample of the average product.

Southern Select, brewed in Houston with Brogniez's recipe and under his direction on the banks of Buffalo Bayou, was by today's standards fairly light fare. The brewmaster himself calculated it to be 4.2 percent alcohol by weight, or about 5.25 alcohol by volume, which is slightly higher than a Budweiser but less than a Bud Light Platinum or Blue Moon Belgian White Ale from MillerCoors. But it struck gold with the taste testers in Ghent, and it endured both as a beer and as a source of Houston pride for much of the next fifty years. It continued to be brewed at the Magnolia until Prohibition, and afterward it was produced under different names by two other breweries, both of which touted the accomplishment of their prize-winning forerunner.

At the time it came off the line, the owners of Houston Ice and Brewing were already enjoying the trappings of their success. In 1909, the company had purchased an adjacent building, renovating its interior in an Italianate style, with fancy tile work and stained-glass windows, for more spacious and luxurious executive offices. "This was when they wanted to live it up," said

Bart Truxillo, a Houston preservationist who now owns this building, the only surviving remnant of the brewery complex, and in 2003 got it declared a Texas Historic Landmark. Truxillo rechristened it the Magnolia Ballroom and began renting it out for special events. Wedding guests today can dance across a floor that once was covered with tables full of Houston businessmen in what was a company-run cafe.

"That's where the bigwigs would meet and have a bottle of beer at lunch," Truxillo says. "It was apparently very popular. It was a grand place to meet and greet and do business. Then Prohibition came along and screwed everything up."

Brogniez was the brewing industry's public face in Houston. But like so many other endeavors in his life, the course of that life was about to be altered—quickly and dramatically. This time, the winds of change had nothing to do with love or family, sickness or health.

For all its celebrated rowdiness, Houston was not immune to the prohibitionist groundswell of the late nineteenth and early twentieth centuries. In late 1905, the ax-wielding Carry Nation herself visited Houston to express her displeasure—to the tune of $750 in damage—with a local drinking establishment that had been named for her. (Houston wasn't unique in this regard, either; as Nation took her rampaging crusade to saloons across the country, besieged barkeeps were known to post signs that read, "All Nations Welcome, Except Carry.") A decade later, a movement to ban booze in England was front-page news in the *Houston Chronicle*, where a sympathetic columnist cited a "solid phalanx of scientists who state that alcoholic beverage is pure poison to the human body."

Wrote columnist Dr. Frank Crane:

> *When I was a boy, about the only people who proclaimed prohibition were cranks, reformers, women and parsons. Newspapers ridiculed it. The learned and the literary smiled at it. The Four Hundred turned up their noses at it. Politicians frowned on it. It seemed to be an outbreak of fanatic, American, ignorant, Puritanical provincialism. Alcohol had captured the imagination of mankind. Literature was soaked with it, from Omar to Dickens. All*

kings and nobles guzzled. Not to poison one's self for sociability was
considered boorish. Things have surely changed. Prohibitionism can hardly
be called an American crankism any more.

A *Chronicle* editorial a day later took the movement's intellectual leader, William Jennings Bryan, to task and called Prohibition "one of the thorns of this age," noting that "it has been gathering strength until a good part of the country is in constant agitation because of it."

One of the agitators was a recently elected U.S. senator from East Texas, Morris Sheppard, who promptly began sponsoring legislation to restrict the liquor industry and would soon introduce what would become the Eighteenth Amendment. As the *Chronicle's* official voice, the editorial suggested Texans would be better off avoiding the fight altogether:

In many states and municipalities it has aroused public feeling to such an
extent that other, and sometimes more vital, issues have been temporarily
lost sight of. In Texas it caused a virtual stagnation of civic affairs for
eight years, and the present chief executive was elected largely because of
a pledge that he would ignore it. No other issue has ever received such a
compliment in Texas.

By this time, however, the national ban was inevitable. Even in Texas, through a patchwork of "local-option" laws, dozens of the state's 264 counties were dry or partially dry. The movement, stemming from legitimate concerns over alcohol abuse and its devastating impact on women and family life, had long since evolved from calling for temperance into insisting on abstinence. Nationally, the dry coalition embraced not just the religiously pious but also the Ku Klux Klan, whose members stoked racist fears about "a black man with a ballot and a bottle." It united unions and other groups hostile to immigrants with industrialists who wanted a sober, more productive labor force. A Houston attorney in May 1915 appealed the death sentence for a man convicted of killing his wife because jurors in the case had been seen drinking beer the night before they rendered their verdict. A majority of Americans were coming to view liquor as an evil that needed to be vanquished.

Then there was the matter of the breweries' behavior. An exercised Adolphus Busch told a Galveston newspaper reporter during a tour of the island in December 1896:

Another farce you have in Texas is your anti-trust law. It is history that trusts make cheaper prices. What are trusts, anyhow? They are combinations of capital. They build cities, undertake gigantic improvements, they are great civilizers. They make progress. Where would all this splendid wharf front be to-day had it not been for a combination of capital. Look at those massive jetties that cost millions of dollars. Look at your biggest business institutions. Are they not all built by a combination of capital. Your laws drive away foreign capital that would develop the resources of this state rapidly. You twist the anti-trust law around so it fits almost any combination of capital. You lock and bar the doors against such capital.

Busch may not have liked the laws, but they hadn't stopped him from doing business in Texas. At the time, he had about $3 million invested here, including his stakes in the Galveston and the American breweries.

Twenty years later, both would forfeit their charters to settle a massive antitrust action brought by the state's attorney general. So would Houston Ice and Brewing and four other Texas-based beer companies.

Attorney General Ben Looney filed suit on January 19, 1915, in Hopkins County, described by the *Dallas Morning News* as "one of the strongest prohibition counties in Texas." By the time he was prepared for trial a year later, Looney had amassed five hundred pounds of incriminating evidence. Some twenty-five thousand pages worth of letters, telegrams and recollected conversations made a convincing case that the companies had formed an illegal monopoly that conspired to set prices, respect territories, support each other in labor disputes and dismantle "all other elements of competition." On Valentine's Day 1899, for example, the brewers, through the auspices of the Texas Consolidated Brewing Association, were alleged to have set minimum wholesale prices for beer, equalized the interest amounts the companies paid on loans, agreed to common language in labor contracts and pledged to support one another during strikes.

Looney's lawyers had compiled so much evidence—its authenticity uncontested by the defense—that when it came time to move the paperwork from Austin to Sulphur Springs for trial, not all of it would fit into a "specimen box" supplied by the Agriculture Department. This record documented the growing alarm over the growing strength of the drys. Brewers were constantly being asked to kick in cash to pay the poll taxes for voters who pledged to vote against local-option dry measures as they arose on ballot after ballot.

"Dear sirs," began a June 23, 1908 letter datelined Houston, "We have a State-wide prohibition fight on our hands and it is fast and furious." The writer asked for a 1 percent levy from the brewers to help fund the fight. Another letter that month, from Autrey, the Houston Ice and Brewing executive, said the appeal for donations was a joint decision: "It was decided that a very large sum is required and that this sum must be available immediately."

The brewing association also used the money to gain influence with lawmakers, staving off an effort to get rid of the poll tax—a distasteful law whose primary purpose was to restrict the voting rights of blacks—because it would hurt the brewers' influence with voters. One letter laying out their strategy is shockingly cynical: "We ought to be doing missionary work among the colored brethren without delay," it said, "as the enemy is hot after them at this moment. Another suggestion: Poll taxes for 1909 can be paid after the first of October, and all possible pressure should be brought to bear upon the antis to induce them to pay same."

It was a concerted effort to thwart local elections far from the towns where the individual breweries were in operation. "I came to Dallas by request of Mr. Autrey," according to one person interviewed on January 7, 1909, "to ascertain the condition of poll tax paying in this city and look over the situation generally." The scout found Fort Worth to be in the "best condition of any city."

But the efforts weren't always successful.

"The unexpected happened in Limestone," began one dispatch, referring to the county that included Mexia, which had just voted itself dry. Brewery representatives had gone through the town and paid off black and white voters alike and calculated they had secured a "200 majority" for the election. But the prohibition measure passed by ten votes. "The only way I can account for the result is that the negroes took their money and retaliated by voting the pro ticket to even up for the treatment received by the negro Dave Johnson that Luedde put out of business after putting him in business."

The antitrust trial, set for January 1916, promised to be a publicity bonanza for prohibitionists, laying bare the back-room shenanigans. It would be a particular spectacle in Hopkins County—"the most overwhelming pro county in this State"—where "the brewers will be more or less a curiosity that far from home."

But when the day of the trial arrived, the brewers had reached a settlement with the state. They would give up their existing charters and agree not to engage in any monopolistic behavior in the future. They paid a total of $276,000 in fines and court costs, a sum equal to $5.9 million today. Galveston Brewing put itself and the entirety of its assets up for public auction in January 1917. Stockholders reserved the right to be part of a new joint stock association.

The fatal blow came soon enough. The Eighteenth Amendment was ratified by the states and enacted into law over the objections of President Woodrow Wilson. January 20, 1920, ushered in one of the strangest periods in American history, a time of mixed signals from the highest branches of government, gangland violence and, most of all, widespread hypocrisy and lawlessness that cut across all of the nation's social strata. It was the era of bootleggers and speakeasies and the citizen-scofflaws who enriched them. Jesse H. Jones, the multifaceted businessman and *Houston Chronicle* publisher and an influential figure in national politics, summed it up this way: "The Prohibition laws and tax laws have made liars and thieves out of ordinary good people."

Prohibition also put good people out of work. Breweries tried to hang on in various ways. The local ones could still sell ice, but that would hardly make up for the lost income. The Magnolia used its insulated buildings for meat storage, but several of its buildings fell into disrepair and collapsed due to a pair of devastating floods. The Galveston Brewing Company reinvented itself as Southern Beverage and started selling a nonalcoholic drink it called Galvo before bottling root beer, ginger ale and other soft drinks under the Triple XXX flag. American seems to have simply been abandoned.

And what of Brogniez? His skill making beer apparently didn't extend to other business endeavors. Another family story holds that when the management at Houston Ice and Brewing tried to reward him for his Grand Prix with some property near downtown, the brewer declined because he didn't know what to do with it. That real estate, near the site of what is now a Sears store, could've left his descendants wealthy people.

"What I've learned is," says Philip Brogniez, "he wasn't a very good businessman, but he could brew some really good beer."

Brogniez was not quite sixty when Prohibition became the law of the land. His livelihood, the pursuit of which had taken him from Brussels to Detroit to Terre Haute to Houston, was gone, and it would be more than a decade before it would return. Brogniez was back to his peripatetic ways.

In 1923, he was again the subject of a glowing newspaper article. Again, the accompanying photographs showed him peering into a microscope at his lab. And again, the tale of his triumph in Ghent was told in soaring language. This time, the story appeared under the headline "Hombres de valer."

"Ilustramos estas páginas con la fotografía de un verdadero hombre de ciencia, el señor Frantz Brogniez, quien tiene a su cargo el departamento químico de la Cía. Cervecera de C. Juárez, S.A., tanto en Bacteriología como en Fermentología."

El Domingo newspaper of El Paso had just introduced its readers to a "true man of science," the head of chemistry at the Juarez Brewery, just over the border in Mexico. Brogniez, who had never learned to drive, was chauffeured to work each day from his new home in El Paso. But he was back in brewing, where he felt he belonged. His beers included a lager that was based on his Southern Select recipe and a darker beer called Richelieu.

"As long as he was brewing beer and had access to the music he liked," says his grandson, "he was a happy camper."

Chapter 4

A Titan Sets His Eyes
on the Grand Prize

The Eighteenth Amendment may have become the law of the land, but the public debate over Prohibition was far from over. It would vex politicians, bureaucrats and law enforcers for most of the next fourteen years. At home, however, it seemed the matter was fairly conclusively settled by the mass of Americans who flagrantly defied the ban as they went about their otherwise law-abiding lives. As documentarian Ken Burns pointed out, it was easier to get a drink during Prohibition than it was after repeal because the speakeasies didn't have to adhere to legally set hours of operation and no government bureaucrat was going to make them check minors for identification. "We are disturbed by the image of Al Capone," said Burns, in reference to the Chicago gangster and the rapid rise of organized crime. But perhaps more troubling, he added, is that for more than a decade, "millions and millions of people were breaking the law." And he wasn't talking about just rumrunners or corrupt cops.

Ed Mergele, who was a child during Prohibition in the largely German community of New Braunfels in the Texas Hill Country, witnessed the everyday ease with which the adults around him carried on their age-old traditions. He recalls going with his father to the bootlegger to pick up bottles of gin and whiskey whenever his parents were planning a party. As for beer, he says, folks made that for themselves with illegal brewing systems they set up in their homes. "Everybody had beer in their house," he says. This home-brew was "terrible stuff," he recalls (which could explain why Mergele never developed a taste for beer as an adult), and there was that one batch that overheated during fermentation and exploded. "It blew out the cabinet doors in the kitchen," he says.

Despite the law, and the potential for goopy messes in the kitchen, few beer drinkers stopped drinking beer.

"Sugar and hops and bottle caps were big sellers in the stores," says Mergele. "All smiles. Everybody just smiled about it."

In 1933, a Mrs. R.C. Patterson asked during a public assembly in Houston's Bohemian Hall "that just one person come forward who could say he had seen or known of anyone who had stopped drinking under prohibition," according to an account in the *Houston Chronicle*. She then vented her frustration with what the law had wrought, saying:

> *When I was a young lady, men did not come to dances with hip flasks. They did not even dare have liquor on their breath. They had some respect for the young ladies they escorted.*
>
> *The speakeasies follow the schools, they follow the residential districts, they spring up, at least on pay day, wherever there are laborers. What had pre-prohibition days to compare with this, with the tragedy that follows the drinking of the stuff these speakeasies serve?*

By then, it was obvious to all but the most recalcitrant drys that the national experiment had caused more problems than it fixed. Some of the same industrialists who'd supported Prohibition now turned against it because the new income tax, to which they were the biggest contributors, was being expected to replace the revenue that once had been covered by excise taxes on liquor. The political conventions of 1932 showed Democrats and Republicans in agreement on the issue, and Franklin Roosevelt won the presidency with repeal as part of his platform. One of his earliest, and easiest, tasks was to get Congress to declare low-alcohol beer—or 3.2 beer, for its alcohol volume by weight—non-intoxicating, allowing its sale in states that hadn't specifically banned the so-called "near beer." In a seventy-two-word message to Congress that March, Roosevelt called for an "immediate modification of the Volstead act" to allow the sale, and "substantial" taxation, of near beer to generate "a proper and much-needed revenue for the government."

The taps reopened on April 7, but not in Texas or the other states that still prohibited near beer. Texans would have to wait until September to legally slake their thirst. As they prepared that August to overturn the beer ban and to vote on the Twenty-first Amendment—the one that would undo the Eighteenth Amendment and formally dismantle Prohibition—a *Chronicle* editorial warned that the state "must not stand in the way of the overwhelming national sentiment. The quicker the eighteenth amendment is repealed the better it will be for everybody concerned. We should speed the inevitable result."

The paper made a compelling case to its readers:

> *The question long since has passed the point where the theoretical merits or demerits of liquor prohibitor laws is involved. When a majority of the people want a thing in this country they must have it. That as a matter of democratic right. But, beyond that, it is obviously folly to believe that a minority of the people, and those resident largely in the rural sections and small towns, can impose a social custom—one that cuts athwart the customs of centuries—on a majority of the people, resident in the cities or anywhere else.*
>
> *After all, law is the expression of public sentiment. To insist on its retention when public sentiment is opposed to it is to invite disaster, regardless of the fact that every person owes it to his country and to democratic government to observe a law whether he likes it or not.*

Even the state's lieutenant governor, Edgar Witt, was on record as saying, "The eighteenth amendment could not be enforced by the king's army and the king's navy."

Then there were the economic benefits promised by repeal, four years into the Great Depression. Roosevelt's interim beer bill alone was expected to generate $100 million to $150 million in federal taxes. The Texas Beer Association predicted twelve to fifteen breweries would open in Texas within three years once the brew was legal here. That would compare with twelve breweries statewide, including the three in Houston and Galveston, that were operating in 1918. The association estimated those breweries would employ 4,500 people, not including "the distributing and clerical departments."

"The indicated consumption of beer in Texas per year is 3,290,000 barrels," executive secretary Alvin Romansky claimed on the eve of the election. "Our figures show that $27 million will be invested in the industry in this state."

Houston Ice and Brewing pledged to reopen, first to distribute "Eastern beer" until its own brew was ready; new president Mumford W. Hoover said the company would employ a total of 1,600 men. Another local official said three other local breweries would have the potential to produce upward of 145,000 barrels. A local ice company also announced plans to convert its plant into a brewery.

Frantz Brogniez, second from left, celebrated the opening of Grand Prize. At right is the prominent Houston lumberman John Henry Kirby; at left are Lieutenant Governor Edgar Witt and Judge Graves. *Collection of Philip Brogniez.*

On August 26, Texas joined the steady anti-Prohibition wave and edged the nation a step closer toward the swift, thirty-six-state majority required to amend the Constitution. Harris County turned out four-to-one in favor of repeal, and the vote was even more lopsided in Houston precincts. The *Chronicle* summed it up in a headline: "City Dripping Wet." Galveston was even wetter, voting seven-to-one for repeal.

Julian A. Weslow, Harris County chairman of the Official Repeal Forces, praised the outcome and boldly predicted a "more sober, better and more prosperous country."

"The victory of liberalism was expected," he said. "All classes joined in amassing this great majority which should finally result in eliminating this troublesome question of prohibition from our politics for a long time to come."

On September 15, beer was back for good. The *Chronicle* reported that steamship lines and railroads had brought in the equivalent of more than nine million bottles of the stuff. The beer companies likewise returned to the newspaper's advertising pages. "If you're glad beer is back you'll be doubly glad when you drink Pabst Blue Ribbon," shouted the first one to run, a lively full-page display. "Good old Blatz" also was back with Old Heidelberg Castle beer, and "Matchless Falstaff" was soon to join. Houston's Nehi Bottling Company wanted everyone to know it would be distributing Country Club Special Beer from Missouri's Goegz Brewing, and Union Transfer and Storages had a contract for Arrow Beer—"Good in '17 and Better today!"—from Baltimore's Globe Brewery. Eagle Beer from New Orleans was now on sale, as was Philadelphia's Black Eagle brand. The most striking ad, for Old Union Lager, featured a sunrise, the Liberty Bell and the Statue of Liberty as it heralded "Re-birth of the Union."

But it was the Anheuser-Busch copywriters, perhaps bored from penning pitches for Budweiser barley malt syrup in red three-pound cans, who now spared no expense in letting "our many friends in the Lone Star State" know just how big a victory they'd achieved:

> *Beer is back! In those three simple words a great American industry has gone back to work. Hands long idle have found new jobs. Faces empty of hope brighten to a new promise. Thousands upon thousands have found honorable livelihood. A vast American market—a new frontier of industry—reopens, bringing sorely needed business to farmers, transportation and to hundreds of other industries. And with it, a new fountain head of tax revenue has arisen to add its dollars gladly to a nation in need.*

Of particular local interest, on September 24, a banner ad proclaimed that the brand-new Southern Brewing Company, "Houston's new half million dollar industry… brewers of Monte Carlo beer," would be in the marketplace soon. Monte Carlo, it noted, would be "fully aged in wood—to be sold in wood." The ad depicted a three-story brew house with immaculately manicured grounds on North Drennan, on Houston's eastside. Several local businesses paid for boxed congratulatory messages, as if they were saluting the town's high school graduates.

Surely Houston was on the verge of another beer boom.

Or not.

While beer guzzling would indeed grow in Texas and across the nation, suds-soaked fortunes would elude most of the city's would-be barons of brew. Houston Ice and Brewing merged with the Galveston Brewery in 1934 and managed to stay in business for twenty-one years before the combined Galveston-Houston Breweries sold its island facilities to Falstaff, another St. Louis–based enterprise. Locally owned Southern Brewing—makers of

Monte Carlo, "The South's Finest," and Alamo beer, sold briefly in Corpus Christi by Ernest Tubb before he hit the country music big time—prospered for two years but wound up bankrupt by the end of the decade. Of the other breweries whose openings were said to be imminent on Election Day, only one ever began production at all.

The Gulf Brewing Company made the city's first batch of legally produced, post-Prohibition beer on October 11, 1933, and began selling it in December after aging it in pitch-lined tanks. Within a few years, Gulf would become one of the South's largest manufacturers of beer. Owned by and built on the grounds of a local oilfield-equipment-supply company, it was the only Houston brewery from this era that would attain anything approaching greatness.

It did so with a beer called Grand Prize.

Ed Mergele's dad jumped into the beer business with gusto. The elder Edwin Mergele had been in lumber originally and by the 1930s was co-owner of a New Braunfels creamery with his brother. With Prohibition tossed onto history's trash heap, the elder Mergele used connections he'd made in St. Louis to secure a deal to distribute Anheuser-Busch products. From there, he expanded quickly and soon had eighteen or nineteen beers in his portfolio. "Grand Prize was his biggest seller," recalled his son, and the thankful proprietors, eager to show their appreciation, invited the entire family over for an all-expense-paid trip to see where that beer was being made.

As Ed recounts the trip today, Dad loaded his wife and son, then eight or nine, into his new, tan 1934-model Ford sedan—"just like the one Bonnie and Clyde got killed in"—and set out for Houston. They spent the night at the plush Rice Hotel, on Gulf's tab, and the next morning they got a private tour of the pristine, million-dollar facilities on Polk Avenue. "It was a beautiful brewery, I remember that," says Ed. Afterward, the brewmaster escorted the Mergeles to the on-site taproom to relax with complimentary beers (root beer for the boy) and a bite to eat.

As they settled in with their drinks, each one served in a dimpled finger-glass stein with a pewter top that opened with a flick of the thumb, they were joined for lunch by a tall, slender man with dark hair. He was thirtyish, just a few years younger than Ed's father, and like Ed's mother, he had grown up in Houston. The two chatted at length about the city, where they'd lived, who they knew in common. When Mrs. Mergele said how much she admired the elegant mug, the dark-haired man called a waiter over and had him wrap it up as a gift. "My dad wasn't impressed," says Ed. "My mother was."

Several years later, after Ed Mergele returned from duty in World War II, he and his mother talked about that trip again, which seemed much more

Gulf Brewing Company's Grand Prize Brewery was built on the grounds of its parent company, Hughes Tool. *Collection of Philip Brogniez.*

significant in hindsight. The dark-haired stranger they'd met was Howard Hughes, the heir in charge of the Hughes Tool Company, which for thirty years owned and operated Houston's biggest brewery. Hughes was soon to be known worldwide as a moviemaker, record-setting aviator and eccentric playboy linked to the likes of Katharine Hepburn. He was well on his way to becoming the world's richest man. But on that day at the brewery, says Ed, "I didn't hear a word about Hollywood or California or anything like that." Just chitchat about who knows who. And the "important person" in the taproom, he declares, was Gulf's septuagenarian brewmaster. And indeed, at that point, more Houstonians were likely to have heard of the brewer than Hughes, who had not yet made his record-setting flight around the globe.

Frantz Brogniez was back in town. The legend of Houston brewing had arrived in October 1932 with plans to get back to work for Houston Ice and Brewing and get ready for Prohibition's repeal. But the Magnolia Brewery complex was near collapse, and the company was undercapitalized. The better-funded men from Hughes Tool saw cash in beer, and they wanted

Brogniez badly. If they couldn't get the rights to the name Southern Select—that belonged to the merged Galveston-Houston Breweries, which would continue to manufacture it—they'd get the man who made it famous and find a way to profit from the prize he'd won. The Grand Prize.

While making beer in Juarez, Mexico, the aging Brogniez had sketched out designs and dreamed of building the ideal modern brewery, one that would take advantage of the latest scientific advances in the craft to which he'd devoted his life. Howard Hughes made that dream come true. "Then, lo and behold," as a Houston newspaper put it, "the money became available and he was told to 'go to it.'" The Hughes Tool men had decided to build a brewery, and they let Brogniez have his way with the design.

Construction began on June 12, and Brogniez worked tirelessly to take the plant from paper to production in less than four months. The bottles that

Frantz Brogniez was given a free hand in designing the Grand Prize brewery for Gulf and lived long enough to oversee the first run of the bottling line. When he died two years later, his son Frantz P. Brogniez took over as brewmaster. *Collection of Philip Brogniez.*

eventually rolled off the line were labeled "Grand Prize," a "full strength lager beer." Sure enough, those bottles also made ample reference to the grand prize that was won in Belgium twenty years earlier.

"Brewed and bottled with the most modern equipment by Frantz H. Brogniez," read a banner in the left top corner of the label. Across the banner in the opposite corner, the message continued, "who won the Grand Prize... Universal and International Brewers Congress, Ghent, 1913."

Gulf Brewing Company made Houston's first legal beer after Prohibition ended. The flagship, Grand Prize, was first brewed by Frantz Brogniez. *Collection of Philip Brogniez.*

But the stress and long hours had taken a toll on Brogniez's health. So had the cigarettes he'd smoked for many years. He died on October 9, 1935, just sixteen days shy of his seventy-fifth birthday. His body was interred in a prominent spot inside the cool, marbled mausoleum at Forest Park Cemetery on Lawndale. Sharing the crypt above him today are the sisters Grymonprez originally from Thourout, Belgium: Alida Mathilde, with whom Brogniez had crossed the Atlantic, and her sister, Alice Albertine, whom Brogniez had married after Alida's death in Detroit in 1903. Alice made the moves to Terre Haute to Houston to El Paso and back to Houston, raising her sister's son and daughter, plus two sons she had with Frantz. All of the Brogniez children would become successful, three after graduating from the prestigious Rice Institute (now Rice University and the alma mater of several notable brewers of the future). Alice died in Houston on February 2, 1963.

After Brogniez's death in 1935, drinkers of the new Grand Prize may or may not have noticed a subtle change to the bottle labels. The artwork remained the same, but the wording in the upper left and right corners was different. Those banners in the upper corners now read, "Brewed and bottled with the most modern equipment by Frantz P. Brogniez from the formula which won the Grand Prize...Universal and International Brewers Congress, Ghent, 1913."

At its peak year of 1947, Gulf Brewing sold just under 483,000 barrels of beer. *Collection of Philip Brogniez.*

Brogniez's oldest son, with a degree in chemical engineering from Rice, had stepped into his father's role as brewmaster at Gulf. His half brother, Fernand, ran the bottling plant. By the following year, Grand Prize was the best-selling beer in Texas.

Like Ed Mergele before her, Susan Lieberman Seekatz was a child when she first set foot on the twelve-acre grounds of the brewery, which was itself tucked away inside the much larger Hughes Tool complex. "It was like a park when you drove in," she says. "They had guinea hens and peacocks walking around. It was beautiful." In photographs from the era, a stand of tall trees fills the frame behind the front gate, and the entrance is accented by palm fronds and signs on either side of the road announcing "GRAND PRIZE." The brew house itself, as Seekatz recalls, was as gleamingly modern as Frantz Brogniez had envisioned a decade and a half before. "It was a sterile operation when we got there," she says. "You could have eaten a meal off the floor. That's how clean it was! Wherever you walked in that brewery, it was immaculate."

For the next fifteen years, her dad made sure it stayed that way. "That's one thing he told me," she says. "It had to be clean because anything can affect taste." And her father—a man who'd been literally born into the brewing business—was an expert in how beer was supposed to taste.

Charles Lieberman was yet another remarkable character in Houston's beer history.

A Georgetown-educated chemist, with a master's degree in chemical engineering, as well as an expert brewer and poet, Lieberman would spend fifteen years making beer for Hughes's Gulf Brewing and winning awards of his own. He would write numerous articles about the trade for the *Brewers Journal*. Every Christmas, he would pen a holiday poem for family and friends on Grand Prize letterhead. His writing would earn him the moniker "poet laureate of the brewing industry." In retirement, he would write an ode to one of Texas's earliest breweries.

Lieberman was born in Allentown, Pennsylvania, on the premises of Jos. Lieberman's Sons, a family brewery with roots dating back to the Civil War, in a state with a prolific brewing history. (The Pennsylvania listing in *American*

Charles Lieberman was another remarkable character in Houston's brewing history. He came to Gulf Brewing Company in 1948 and made Grand Prize beer until the brewery was sold in 1963. *Collection of Susan Lieberman Seekatz.*

Breweries II goes on for more than sixty pages; by comparison, Texas takes up fewer than six.) Lieberman started out scrubbing floors in the brewery, which was then run by his dad and uncle. At twenty-four, he apprenticed at the Widman Brewing Company of Bethlehem, Pennsylvania, and later worked at the Neuweiler Brewing Company back in Allentown. His career advanced quickly, and in 1937 he joined a competing brewery, Horlacher, where he worked for more than a decade and rose to the positions of head brewmaster and plant manager. There, Lieberman revived one of Horlacher's pre-Prohibition beers, the Nine Months Old Perfection. It was similar to traditional India pale ales, which were made to endure long sea voyages from Britain to its soldiers stationed in India, and Perfection was in fact aged for nine months before being packaged in amber bottles and exported to the sophisticates of Chicago and New York.

Eventually, opportunity called from down south, and he left Pennsylvania to become an assistant brewmaster at the much larger Gulf Brewing. Lieberman, his wife, son and ten-year-old daughter, Susie, arrived in Houston in 1948. Like the Brogniez family before them, the Liebermans quickly took to their new home in humid Texas, even if they didn't fall completely under the sway of its customs. One of the first things Charles Lieberman did was to take down the "Colored" and "Mexican" signs that

Tanks at Gulf Brewing Company's Grand Prize Brewery. *Collection of Philip Brogniez.*

directed brewery workers to the separate entrances and facilities. This admirable and progressive stand raised eyebrows but didn't harm his career, and in 1950, Lieberman was promoted to vice-president and brewmaster. But he never became just a manager of the business; the beer always came first. His daughter recalls that he maintained a laboratory next to his office.

"I asked him, 'What's the best beer?'" she recalls. "He said it was your freshest beer. He said your local beer is the freshest."

The beer is even fresher when it comes straight from the tanks, and most microbreweries these days well understand the marketing appeal of hosting tours in hope the happy visitors will tell their friends and keep them in mind the next time they stop off for a six-pack. The makers of Grand Prize got this instinctively and from the outset invited the public over for free tours, followed, according to a press account, by trips "to the rathskeller, too, a beautiful little taproom." The brewery quickly became a destination for visiting celebrities and dignitaries as well. An early photograph shows the elder Brogniez entertaining Lieutenant Governor Witt and the lumber baron John Henry Kirby, with a pewter-topped stein hoisted high

In December 1949, Lieberman introduced a product called Pale Dry Grand Prize. Beer geeks today, accustomed to slick brewery websites that provide precise technical specs of their favorite craft beers, from the level of alcohol by volume to the specific hop and malt varieties used in production, might find the Pale Dry's brewmaster a bit imprecise in his description of this "beer you have been waiting for." But it's a colorful account and more likely his own work rather than the product of a publicist. In a promotional brochure stamped with his signature, Lieberman praises the "sparkling light amber glow topped by a creamy white billowing froth...comparable to the very best and highest-priced brews on the market." He boasts of a "subtlety of flavor that always invites you to another swallow."

And he does provide some insight into the brewing process, however general. In his own words:

> *Only the very top grades of barley malt, the finest of hops from the selected blossoms of the female vines, and the purest variety of brewers' rice are used. An additional routine examination by a recognized leading malt beverage laboratory insures constant uniformity of this superior brew... Slow fermentation by the priceless pure strain of cultured yeast, and long aging under the careful scrutiny of the ever-watchful staff of brewers and technicians bring out the best from the expertly selected ingredients. Only the pure natural fermentation gas is used to enliven this brew. Through*

A commemorative keg recognizing a milestone for "great tastin' Grand Prize." *Collection of Susan Lieberman Seekatz.*

an elaborate process this carbon dioxide is removed, collected, washed, compressed, and stored. It is then allowed to seep slowly back into the mammoth aging tanks in tiny bubbles through the uniquely designed cylindrical porous stones. By this method the carbonation can be precisely controlled so that this PALE DRY GRAND PRIZE Beer always has the exact amount of life and glitter to give it that delightful zest.

The brochure ends on an emphatic note: "The people of Texas can be proud of this premium-brewed beer. We know you will like it!"

Chapter 5

Heady Days in Houston and Galveston

As Hughes's fame grew, so did the cachet he attached to Grand Prize. His name was frequently referenced in public mentions of the brewery, however hands-off his actual involvement with the enterprise may have been. His aura added a bit of glamour at a time when this is what Houstonians were craving. It was a period of conspicuous prosperity and optimism brought on by the fantastic growth of the oil, gas and refining industry. The legendary Texas journalist Stanley Walker captured the spirit of the times in a sprightly snapshot. The mid-decade essay in the *New York Times* is affectionate in tone, though it's never hard to tell when the writer's tongue is tucked firmly in cheek. Walker describes Houston as a "dynamic, unstoppable city." Accompanied by a cartoon drawing of a tall-hatted Texan in a three-piece suit, smiling comfortably under a menacing sun, the article was occasioned by the city's boast that it had conquered a challenge more daunting than building the Ship Channel. The Chamber of Commerce had again laid claim to the title of "The Most Air-Conditioned City," citing statistics showing 0.271 tons of air conditioning for each of the city's 800,000 residents:

Even the skeptics—and there are many die-hard, mossy-horned, fundamentalist, old-fashioned Texans who have long held that no good can come of monkeying with the weather—are beginning to admit that there does seem to be a little more happiness per square inch. Men and women still in middle life can remember the time, only a few years back, when a visit to Houston in the long blistering summer was an ordeal to be endured only if there was a good chance of grabbing some of the city's famous money.

"I can remember," says a prominent Texas statesman who perspires easily, "when I would have to go to Houston in the summer to discuss grave issues. At night I would turn on the big overhead fan in my hotel room. That didn't help much. I could only get relief by soaking the sheets in the bathtub and sleeping between them. It's a wonder it didn't kill me. It would give a goat pneumonia within an hour."

Further alluding to the oil wealth that had already cemented Houston's image in popular culture, Walker notes that it had "more millionaires per cubic yard than any comparable city, if there is such a thing as a comparable city," and he suggests slyly that, with "air conditioning approaching the saturation point," these must be the "happiest and most clear-visioned millionaires on earth." He also includes a humorous take on that tension, evident from its earliest days, between the city's natural proclivities and its commitments to behave. He writes:

Virtually every church of any importance in Houston has put in some form of air conditioning in the course of the last few years. One local school of thought holds that this will mean a great upturn in religious interest and a consequent improvement in general morality. Those who doubt this theory point out that the juke joints, the beer parlors and the liquor stores also have been air-conditioned, so that things will probably stay about where they are. However, the people on both sides of the fence will be more comfortable.

Gulf Brewing got the celebrity treatment in other ways. When the company announced in late 1950 that sales of its new Pale Dry were up 40 percent over the same period the previous year and that it was launching a new advertising campaign to goose sales in the coming year, the *Houston Press* gave the story front-page play, under the banner headline: "PALE DRY IS THE REASON WHY." With Charles Lieberman in charge of the brew house, Grand Prize brought home international medals in 1952 (from Antwerp), 1953 (Paris) and 1954 (Munich). For the 1953 Cross of Honor, Grand Prize was cited for "clarity, bouquet and taste." By 1954, the year Lieberman was promoted to vice-president, Gulf had sold 6.5 million barrels of "grand tastin' Grand Prize." Though annual sales had peaked in 1947 at 483,000 barrels, the brewery was still pumping out upward of a quarter-million barrels every year, shipping kegs, cans and bottles across Texas and into Oklahoma, New Mexico and Louisiana as well.

Charles Lieberman, second from right, hosts a group for beers at the hospitality room at the Grand Prize Brewery. *Collection of Susan Lieberman Seekatz.*

Yet Gulf was not immune from growing pressures in the beer business. About seven hundred breweries opened in the United States upon the fall of Prohibition, about half as many as were in operation before. That number steadily declined in the decades that followed. "We have to scrap for every bottle of beer we sell these days," a Gulf spokesman told the *Wall Street Journal* during the United States Brewers Foundation's 1950 meeting. Increased capacity built up after the fall of Prohibition was now meeting a suddenly falling national demand. Consumption had climbed to fifty-three million barrels in 1940, from thirty-two million in 1934, but peaked at around eighty-five million barrels in 1947–48. The smaller local and regional breweries were particularly vulnerable once demand fell in 1949. "A lot of old and inefficient plants probably won't be able to compete," an unnamed "big East Coast beer maker" told the *Journal*. "They'll probably have to get out. Some already have."

One of those making an early exit from the post-Prohibition gold rush was A.M. Arnold, a Houston builder and contractor. "With the cessation of national prohibition in 1933 he thought money could be made in the beer brewing business," according to a ruling by the Fifth U.S. Circuit Court of Appeals in 1941. The order was issued in a bankruptcy case, a good clue as to how things turned out for his Southern Brewing Company. Arnold was represented in his appeal by the Houston attorney Leon Jaworski, who would become famous to future generations as the Watergate special prosecutor, and the Fifth Circuit offers a somewhat detailed account of the challenges that confronted Arnold's Houston startup.

Arnold secured a charter to make beer in July 1933 and incorporated as Southern Brewing with his son-in-law, Otto, and a brewer named Souza. Arnold put up the initial $50,000 capital, and the business prospered for a time, showing a $97,000 surplus at the end of 1936. "The business then began to lose money," according to the court. In May 1938, Arnold gave his stock to Otto, who assumed management of the brewery. In October, he foreclosed on the plant, bought it at public auction and leased it to the corporation, "which continued to operate there without any apparent difference." The tactics weren't enough to stave off bankruptcy six months later.

The court found no fraud or mismanagement in Arnold's dealings with the business and with his associates. Left unstated is simply how tough the business could be. A Texas beer man laid out the challenge for the *Journal* in 1950: "At present Texas gets about half its beer from outside the state. We can't hope to keep out these nationally advertised beers, but maybe we can bring the percentage up to sixty/forty in our favor." Or, as a representative of one of those big national breweries told the paper during the same meeting, "The industry is just getting back to normal." By 1951, San Antonio's rapidly growing Lone Star and Pearl breweries had each surpassed Gulf and were solidifying their dominance in Texas.

Even a teenage Susie Lieberman recognized the tough competitive challenges her dad and his colleagues faced at Gulf. The business pressures took a toll on labor relations as well. During a panel discussion at the Brewers Foundation 1948 meeting, Gulf's executive vice-president, Dwight Thomas, encouraged his peers to take an active interest in the lives of their employees and to avoid halfhearted training programs. "We can manage machines, but we must teach and train people," he was quoted in the *Times* as saying. "Men, like machines, need physical adjustments, but they also need to be adjusted mentally, emotionally and spiritually."

This progressive management attitude would soon be tested. As early as 1956, the executive vice-president of Hughes Tool, Noah Dietrich, was denying rumors that it had put Gulf Brewing on the block. The plant was still in operation two years later, but it had lost its 25 percent local market share and launched a new beer as part of a comeback bid. This new "Flavor Harmony" product, which had been under development under Lieberman's direction for a year and a half, was to be released with "saturation" advertising that included, of all things, a two-and-a-half-minute jingle written specifically for the campaign.

But not even the "GP Polka" could squelch the jitters about a possible sale. In 1959, some seventy employees represented by the Brewery Workers Union and International Association of Machinists went on strike and held out for twenty weeks, leading to shortages of Grand Prize in its home market. A sticking point in negotiations was a so-called "successor clause" offering job protection in the event the brewery were sold.

Ultimately, the two sides got a contract in place, and labor and management pledged to work together for "the aggressive promotion of sales." But Grand Prize was soon to fade from history.

Hughes Tool cut its losses in 1963. The company founded by Howard Hughes's father announced in March that it was leasing the brewery to the Theodore Hamm Brewing Company of Saint Paul, Minnesota. Rather than a flagship with strong local roots, the Houston plant would now be a regional branch, one of four breweries under control of what was then the largest

A mug stamped with the signature of brewmaster Charles Lieberman. *Collection of Susan Lieberman Seekatz. Photographed by Ronnie Crocker.*

supplier of beer in the western United States. Hamm's president, William C. Figge, came to town and pledged to invest $1 million in factory upgrades. "The secret to a beer is the process that is used," he explained.

There were no immediate plans to push the plant beyond its current capacity of 500,000 barrels a year, but M.E. Montrose, a Hughes senior vice-president, pointed out to a group of business leaders at the Houston Club that there was plenty of room for expansion in the future. He and Figge also announced that a dozen or so workers had been added to the 110-employee payroll and more would be hired soon.

In October, the company came out with a full-page ad of its own: "Now brewed in Texas! Premium Hamm's Beer, at popular Texas prices." The beer, it said, "comes straight to you from one of Texas' most modern breweries."

True enough, the brewery had a Texas address, 5301 Polk Avenue in Houston. But it was no longer a Texas brewery. "Our brewery in Houston will be another step down the road toward national distribution," Figge said. "We hope to see before too long complete national distribution for Hamm's." The Minnesotans brought in their director of marketing to replace Gulf's general manager, James A. Delmar, who would continue with Hughes Tool as an assistant vice-president and director of industrial relations.

Charles Lieberman would make an even bigger transition—and unlike Brogniez before him, he would enjoy a long and productive life after his brewing career was over. When Gulf closed, Lieberman went to work for NASA as a safety and training director at Johnson Space Center for two and a half years before moving to New York as a consultant to the brewing industry. In 1989, he received what his daughter calls "his most cherished honor," a lifetime achievement award from the Master Brewers Association of the Americas. He also made the national *Who's Who in Chemistry*.

In retirement, Lieberman continued to enjoy traveling and learning new things. These were lifelong passions he'd instilled in his daughter from a young age, whether by helping with a school science project on the interaction between hops and malts or supporting her studies abroad in Mexico and Spain. She'd tagged along, too, on so many Saturday-morning brewery checks that in her seventies she can still recall the sweet aromas of the brew house. While her dad was in his nineties, Seekatz accompanied him on a cruise to the Galapagos Islands and a walking tour of the Greek Acropolis.

"He was quite a man," she says. In fact, she attributes her father's death in 2008, less than three months before his one hundredth birthday, to injuries he suffered when a man fell on him during an exercise class.

Lieberman left his remarkable body to science.

A sign posted on the wall of a deteriorating brick and masonry building that faces Church Street in Galveston, between 33rd and 34th, beckons passersby with the promise of "Renovation Falstaff Brewery" and a telephone number to call for more information. Or, rather, it would beckon if it weren't almost totally obscured by an overgrown bush. The sign outside the brewery that opened to great fanfare in 1897 and was an island landmark until it was idled in 1982 has yet to spark any renovation. Like the beer factories of Houston, this one, too, had been buffeted by the unsympathetic cycles of growth and decline, most recently as a regional plant for St. Louis–based Falstaff. Unlike most of its contemporaries in Houston, however, this one offers a tangible touchstone to a special era. You just have to use your imagination.

In 2002, when Ralph W. Stenzel Jr. and a friend went inside the abandoned building and began sweeping it out, they found remnants of the Galveston Brewing Company as it existed when Adolphus Busch and William Lemp had teamed with local investors to build it in the 1890s: unbroken panes of an original window, a rusting tank, stairs with iron railings and a sign over

The abandoned remnants of the old Galveston Brewery, which most recently was operated by Falstaff until it closed in 1982. *Photo by Ronnie Crocker.*

a doorway that read "Brewhouse." At the end of each cleanup session, they would repair upstairs to what once had been a rooftop hospitality room to pop open a cold beer and, from the comfort of lawn chairs they'd brought with them, enjoy a cityscape vista that extended to the Gulf of Mexico.

Nearly forty years earlier, a Santa Fe Railroad man named Bill Crocker, with his new bride, Betty, had enjoyed the hospitality there, along with pitchers of freshly brewed Falstaff beer. Waiters, he recalls, never let their glasses become empty. The couple were in the company of some electricians who had been hired to work on a nuclear-powered ship docked in the barrier island's port for an overhaul.

The brewery buildings are weather-beaten survivors in a city that knows a thing or two about perseverance, from the great storms of 1900 and 1915 through Hurricanes Carla, Alicia and Ike and the man-made catastrophe of Prohibition. Stenzel, whose great-uncle owned the brewery for a time in the 1950s, committed the story of its history to paper in 1999 in a reverent work filled with vintage photographs, legal documents, correspondence on official letterhead and copies of old advertising displays for the range of beers and soft drinks that had been brewed and bottled there. A painted postcard shows an oversized bottle of High Grade, "the beer that's liquid food," drawn into the surf in front of the seawall that was built to protect Galveston; a

Postcard for High Grade Beer highlights the Galveston Seawall, which was built in the wake of the devastating 1900 hurricane. *Collection of Ralph W. Stenzel Jr.*

photo from 1938 shows a line of union-organized brewery workers attired in white shirts, pants and hats marching in a downtown Labor Day parade; an array of calendars, glasses, six-pack boxes and crates, key chains and other tchotchkes promote the beers made by these union men.

The illustrations help Stenzel tell the story of the brewery and how it adapted to an ever-evolving series of challenges. For example, it wasn't until the island was able to guarantee access to artesian well water from the mainland that the Busch men were convinced they could build a successful business there. When they decided they could, in 1895, the city embraced their plans with enthusiasm. Responding to rising prohibitionist sentiment in the early twentieth century, marketers promoted High Grade's low alcohol content as "not enough to hurt anyone." Rather, advertisements noted that one would have to drink fifteen glasses of the beer before they'd ingested the same amount of alcohol as from a single glass of whiskey. One hailed High Grade as "a wholesome and natural temperance drink (containing only $3\frac{1}{2}$ per cent of alcohol), that promotes digestion and enriches the blood. It is a thousand times better for the human stomach and nerves than dyspepsia creating concoctions like coffee and pink tea."

In 1913, the brewery expanded with a $100,000 bottling house that could fill and label thirty thousand bottles every day. "We have spared no expense in our plans for the plant," Stenzel quotes brewery manager I.A. Stein as saying, "and expect to be able to handle our increased business with ease." Those days of growth were numbered—for the local beer barons, they always were—but the Galveston brewery managed to survive both the attorney general's lawsuit and then Prohibition by producing soft drinks. New owners and new names followed. First, it was the Southern Beverage Company, which made a nonalcoholic and not very popular drink called Galvo; in 1927, it became the Triple XXX Brewing Company and eventually distributed root beers, ginger ales and other sodas in thirty-five states and sold them at some one hundred "thirst stations." Despite this success, financial problems mounted, and in 1933, the company's assets were again offered up at a courthouse auction. They went for $117,825.32.

But there were eager buyers who sensed opportunity in the imminent fall of Prohibition, and the plant underwent a series of rapid changes in 1933 and 1934. Less than a month after the public sale, the assets were deeded over to the reincarnated Galveston Brewing Company, which was in turn sold to Robert Autrey, formerly of the Houston Ice and Brewing Company that ran the shuttered Magnolia Brewery, in August. The following March, Autrey rechristened the enterprise the Galveston-Houston Breweries.

Following Prohibition, when Houston Ice and Brewing Company was unable to reopen its Magnolia Brewery, its former vice-president bought the Galveston complex and renamed the company Galveston-Houston Breweries. The new company began making beers with their pre-Prohibition names. *Collection of Ralph W. Stenzel Jr. Photographed by Ronnie Crocker.*

Stenzel writes that the Houstonian did much more than change the name:

> *A lot of time and money was spent to design, construct and assemble the right kind of equipment for the manufacture of the new beer. Every single piece of brewing equipment at the plant was new, modern and the best that could be purchased at the time. Included in the new equipment were copper brew kettles, a rice cooker, malt storage bins, large steel lagering vats lined with ammaut to insure purity and flavor, all bronze pumps and a white keg racking machine.*

Five months later, Autrey and his son, Herbert, president of the new company, and their straight-from-Hamburg brewer, Karl Brehm, had "the famous Magnolia beer" back on the shelves. That would be followed by another brand well known among Texas tipplers, Southern Select.

The good times were back. Galveston-Houston made 123,000 barrels of beer in 1936. At its peak in 1948, production surpassed 458,000 barrels.

A Heady History of Brewing in the Bayou City

In addition to devoting fifteen years to researching the brewery, Stenzel, who is the mayor of Santa Fe, a mainland town in Galveston County, amassed quite a collection of memorabilia. Although he has sold some of it lately, all manner of Magnolia, Southern Select and Triple XXX bottles, cans and knickknacks share space on his well-stocked bookshelves in his one-hundred-year-old farmhouse off one of the main highways through town. His collection includes a pair of brass beer taps his wife found at an estate sale and an embroidered Southern Select jacket worn by a deliveryman with a notably small frame. A Magnolia crate sits in the living room, and a decorative plate for the original American Brewing Association hangs on a wall in the kitchen. Stenzel's favorite item, a beautifully illustrated promotional calendar from 1941, adorns one end of the dining room; on the opposite wall hangs a watercolor painted by a friend based on a vintage photograph of the brewery at the time his uncle owned it.

These relics are wistful reminders of a colorful and long-overlooked era. The photographs Stenzel chose for his book—Southern Select billboards over the Pleasure Pier, bathing beauties on Splash Day floats sponsored by the brewery—present an image of a Galveston that, as is said of New Orleans, appears to be a "city that care forgot." But the book doesn't shy from the starker facts about the beer business. A prospectus prepared by his uncle in 1954 for a stock sale that never occurred shows the brewery hadn't turned a profit since 1951. Output declined steadily after its 1948 peak, falling to 223,000 barrels in 1953. (Hughes's Gulf Brewing in Houston was on a similar trajectory, these records show, peaking at 483,000 barrels in 1947, before falling to 266,000 barrels in 1953.)

Ralph Stenzel, whose great-uncle owned the Galveston brewery for a time in the 1950s, has amassed an impressive collection of artifacts and photographs. *Collection of Ralph W. Stenzel Jr.*

Like Gulf, Galveston-Houston would not endure as an independently owned brewery. But Edward Stenzel, a certified public accountant and the brother of Ralph Stenzel's grandfather, gave it one last go. In October 1953, he bought out Herbert Autrey and the other stockholders for $2.7 million and then quickly recouped all but $1,000 by tapping cash assets to pay back the loans.

Ed Stenzel moved quickly to build the Southern Select brand, spending a half-million dollars on marketing the first year and putting two new varieties on the market. One, Superlite, was lighter in color and calories and more heavily carbonated; it targeted women and sold well in restaurants. The so-called Special version was fuller of body and marketed toward a more traditional consumer. Writes Ralph Stenzel, "The Special beer was the most popular in locations where men, especially 'working' men were customers."

Southern Select sales continued to slide, however, and as they did, tensions grew between the union and the brewery owner. This mirrored the problems the Gulf management soon would have with its workforce, but with a nasty twist. In Galveston, the ill will was said to have been so great that Ed Stenzel drew actual gunfire while being driven to work from his home in Houston.

Texans weren't drinking less beer, but they were switching their allegiances to the Lone Star and Pearl breweries in San Antonio, which collectively doubled in size during this same period and by 1953 were selling 1.3 million

Ralph Stenzel's great-uncle tried to boost sales of Southern Select with the introduction of Superlite. *Collection of Ralph W. Stenzel Jr.*

Cowboy-themed point-of-sale advertising for Southern Select. *Collection of Ralph W. Stenzel Jr.*

barrels between them. Both Gulf and Galveston-Houston would succumb. Stenzel got out first, selling to Falstaff in 1956 for $1.3 million in cash. Southern Select beer would be brewed for a time by Pearl before it, too, vanished for good.

When it was gone, so was the Brogniez family recipe that had traveled from Belgium to the United States to Mexico and back.

Falstaff's Galveston operations would grow enough by 1965 to warrant a plant expansion, and the tours it began offering in 1959 drew good-sized crowds and lots of out-of-state guests. But brewing wasn't to last on the island, and Stenzel chronicled the declines that began in 1972 when Falstaff sold a majority of its stock and accelerated in 1977 when the remainder was sold: "For a while, a beer called Steinbrau was brewed and packaged under the Pearl Beer label in Galveston and in San Antonio. Financial difficulties finally caused the Falstaff Brewery in Galveston to officially close in 1982."

By then, a long-familiar name in brewing had returned to the area, and there didn't seem to be room for anyone else.

Chapter 6

Houston Becomes a Bud Town

Hamm Brewing came to Houston in 1963 promising jobs and a "special taste just built for a Texas thirst." During its first full year after leasing the former Grand Prize Brewery, the Minnesota company posted more than $124 million in overall sales, making it the nation's eighth-largest beer supplier. But during much of Hamm's brief tenure in Texas, executives were busy entertaining suitors. Bidding for the company heated up in 1965, and Molson and Rheingold each made a run at Hamm before Heublein gobbled it up that October in a stock deal valued at $62 million. Heublein, based in Connecticut, added Hamm's beers to a product portfolio that ranged from Smirnoff vodka to A-1 steak sauces.

Such a merger was hardly an aberration. Consolidation, foreseen more than a decade earlier, was marching across the brewing industry and sweeping away regional brands in its path. In October 1967, Hamm was gone from Houston, too, and Hughes Tool Company, which owned the brewing facilities and the twelve acres they sat on, began converting the property to other manufacturing uses. The factory that once rolled out "grand tastin' Grand Prize" by the hundreds of thousands of barrels would soon be turning out gear boxes for Hughes helicopters.

The task got underway shortly. Around 2:30 p.m. on February 12, 1968, a welder's spark at one of the former brewery buildings ignited the cork lining that once had kept fresh beer chilled below forty degrees. Within minutes, Houston firefighters had a four-alarm blaze on their hands, and it just kept getting worse. "Once that cork gets on fire, you can't get to it," James Delmar, a Hughes executive who had been the last general manager at Grand Prize,

A fire in 1968 destroyed most of what remained of the former Grand Prize Brewery. *Photo by Curtis McGee/*Houston Chronicle.

told the media. "It was powder-dry. With all the openings and the breeze, it was a wind tunnel."

By nightfall, all that remained of the Texas landmark was its five-story brew house. And on June 3, the Atlas Demolishing Company began taking that down, too. It was an unsentimental end for a once-beloved local business, marked by a single-paragraph brief in the newspaper. But making beer had always been a tough trade, and Grand Prize was hardly the only brewery to rise and then fall. Nationally, the following years would see many more fall than rise. A handful of brewery giants, led by Anheuser-Busch, would dominate the domestic beer scene for decades. An even more shocking shakeup awaited early in the next century.

This new era broke ground in Houston in 1963.

In 1877, America's ten largest breweries produced barely 1 million barrels of beer between them. At the top of the list was George Ehret, one of five New York City–based breweries then ranked among the top ten. No. 32 on this list, with reported sales of 44,961 barrels, the E. Anheuser and Company's Brewing Association wasn't even the biggest in St. Louis. But this modest family firm, owned at that time by Eberhard Anheuser, was about to begin a transformation that would make it the world's largest beer company and the most identifiably American.

This rapid, relentless expansion began in earnest after Anheuser's death in 1880, when his son-in-law Adolphus Busch took charge of the company and renamed it the Anheuser-Busch Brewing Association. In 1895, Anheuser-Busch was producing more than 700,000 barrels annually and shipping its beers—including one that Busch named for a town in Bohemia called Budweiser—across the country and overseas. During its peak pre-Prohibition year, 1913, the company made 1.5 million barrels.

Busch built or heavily funded several other U.S. breweries to support his global empire. Among them were four in Texas: the American Brewery in Houston, the Galveston Brewery, Lone Star in San Antonio and the Texas Brewing Company in Fort Worth. His investments in Texas, already valued at more than $3 million by the turn of the century, would include real estate, hotels and an ice company in Waco that at one time was one of the largest west of the Mississippi River.

His roots in the state were as deep as his ambitions were wide.

The youngest of twenty-one children (twenty of them sons) born to a German timber man, Busch was eighteen when he set out for America in 1855. He married Anheuser's daughter, Lilly, in 1861, and after the Civil War—during which he served a short but accomplished stint in the Union army—he joined the family brewing business. Once he took over, Busch pushed hard to expand, moving the company's beers into the Southwest by horseback and then by refrigerated railcars. The line of products grew to include Original Budweiser, Pilsener, Old Burgundy, the Faust Beer and other brands. Busch was the first brewer to pasteurize beer and the first to put it in bottles. He worked with competitors to set prices. He drove into Mexico, South America and even Australia. Then he conquered Europe and continued to broaden the company's distribution horizon until, as one of his biographers has noted, "the sun never sets on the name of Anheuser-Busch."

By the time of his death while vacationing at his estate in Germany in 1913, Busch was personally worth $50 million—he'd be a billionaire today—and had built Anheuser-Busch into a powerhouse. The company was valued at $31.5 million and had generated $3.8 million in profits that year.

He was mourned in Dallas, where his commercial endeavors ranged from a cold-storage plant to the twenty-two-story Hotel Adolphus. The flags were ordered to half-staff for three days.

"Mr. Busch was the most extraordinary and splendid character I have ever met during my long hotel experience," the Adolphus manager, Alvah R. Wilson, told the *Dallas Morning News*. "His intellectuality and personality was such as to create an admiration so profound as to absolutely beggar description...When one pauses to consider the man—the almost superhuman intellect which controlled interests with ramifications as extensive as those of the Anheuser-Busch concern—it is truly bewildering."

One can only wonder what the industrialist would've thought about a fully automated beer-manufacturing plant run mostly by machines that measure out grains and hops automatically and monitor, via underwater cameras, the secret workings of yeast floating in the bowels of giant fermentation tanks. Doubtless, he would be pleased that this marvel of modern brewing, still bearing his name, could pump out nearly ten times as much beer—most of it something called Bud Light—annually as the entire company did during the last year of his life. The audacity of it alone would've made him proud.

But he probably wouldn't be surprised at all to learn that his descendants had decided to build this modern plant down in Texas. He'd built a few there himself.

In the summer of 1964, the Anheuser-Busch Inc. directors, led by Adolphus Busch's grandson and attended by his great-grandson, held their first-ever regular board meeting in Houston so they could see firsthand their $32 million construction project. Work had begun the year before on a 105-acre tract on the city's industrial

Vintage Anheuser-Busch advertising appeals to the Texas mystique. *Photo by Ronnie Crocker.*

and sparsely populated far-eastern edge. A giant steel frame was already rising from the flatlands when the executives arrived. The downtown skyline was smaller and seemed a lot farther away than it does today. The plant, the fifth nationally to operate under the company's universally recognized eagle logo, would be in operation by early the next year with an initial annual capacity of 900,000 barrels.

That wouldn't make it the biggest—Anheuser-Busch's home brewery in St. Louis covered seventy city blocks and had an annual capacity of seven million barrels—but it would be far bigger than any built in Houston before. And Houstonians, then at work on the Astrodome a few miles away, had a thing for big projects.

Bud was the big player now. In 1966, Houston became a Bud town.

Shortly after noon on a weekday in early December forty-five years later, the hospitality room of the Houston plant is filled with children's toys for soldiers' families at Fort Hood and tables of gear emblazoned with Budweiser logos to raise money for more gifts. At 3:00 p.m., the day-shift workers will be invited in for an after-work holiday happy hour with snacks, fresh beer and a chance to bid on the items in a silent auction. The graveyard shift had its happy hour at 7:00 a.m. and the evening crew at 11:00 p.m. the night before. At the busy brewery, even employee appreciation and charity fundraising must be kept to a tight schedule.

"We expect the same number of brews on the eight-hour shifts of midnights as we do today," says Dave Maxwell, who was brewmaster of the Houston plant for a decade before taking over the packaging operation a year and a half earlier.

Maxwell and Dave Cohen, who succeeded him as brewmaster, are among the six-hundred full-time employees and one hundred-plus part-timers who will produce and ship 12.5 million barrels—a mind-boggling 387.5 million gallons—of beer this year. That's enough to fill more than four billion twelve-ounce bottles. Crews work around the clock mixing tons of malt, rice and hops with upward of a billion gallons of water. Other workers take all this Budweiser and Bud Light, ZiegenBock and Michelob and pump it into cans, kegs and bottles that are then loaded onto the big trucks that pull out onto Loop 610 en

Dave Cohen (left) is the brewmaster at the Anheuser-Busch InBev plant in Houston. His predecessor, Dave Maxwell, runs the packaging operation. *Photo by Ronnie Crocker.*

route to a network of wholesalers for distribution throughout Texas and into limited areas in its border states, Mexico, Central America and Puerto Rico. Making sure specific brands roll out when needed and in the right combination of package sizes requires careful planning and nearly flawless execution.

The work starts with a small team inside an air-conditioned control room with a glass-wall view of the red-tiled brew house below. In this comfortable environment, workers monitor three banks of computer screens, some filled with murky underwater images and others with colored data points decipherable only to them. They key in recipes and grain poundage to get the giant mash vessel going and keep track of a host of chemical levels. They watch yeast by remote-controlled video and make certain all electrical and mechanical systems are running the way they're supposed to, calling in technicians whenever something doesn't register correctly.

"We're just along for the ride and to make sure it all does what it's supposed to do," says John Swiercz, who has worked at the plant for thirty-two years and remembers when it was much more dependent on manual labor.

During his tenure, Bud Light has become by far the biggest-selling brand in Texas; 55 to 60 percent of the beer made at the Houston plant today rolls out in its distinctive blue and white packaging.

After a week of primary fermentation, the beer here is piped into huge lagering tanks atop a bed of beechwood. This oft-cited "beechwood aging" involves packing the soft, light-colored wood in curled strips of about eighteen inches apiece into long, stainless-steel "chip torpedoes" and wheeling them over to the tanks, where the beechwood strips are loaded in by hand before the beer is pumped in. As the yeast falls to the bottom inside the tank, it will thus cover a larger surface area and interact more efficiently with the beer. The wood is thoroughly cleaned beforehand and doesn't impart any special flavor, although Cohen says the process can give the beer a cleaner finish. At any rate, it means the product is ready for shipment after just three weeks in this second stage of fermentation. When the beer is ready for packaging, the control room routes it to the proper filling lines.

Automation may ease the logistical load of such a complex industrial operation, but Cohen says he and his teams of assistants have to rely on their brewing skills and training to make sure the beers turn out the same, batch after batch, day after day. Beer, like wine, is made from agricultural products that are sensitive to droughts, floods and other variations in the weather, but brewers don't have the option available to vintners of letting

Beechwood shavings are loaded into these "torpedoes" and delivered to the lagering tanks at the Anheuser-Busch InBev plant in Houston. Beechwood aging doesn't impart any flavor, but it does make fermentation more efficient by increasing the surface area that yeast has to interact with the beer as it ages. *Photo by Ronnie Crocker.*

the condition of the grapes dictate how a particular vintage will taste. There is a specific recipe for each Budweiser product, each with its own set grain bill, hops quantity and a target amount of bitterness. But the brewer's art involves knowing how to adjust the boil in the brew kettle or subtly tweak the fermentation to bring those ingredients in line. Every batch is taste-tested for quality control.

"It's still that hands-on brewing, using your sensory skills to make sure the beer comes out the same," says Cohen.

As Maxwell leads a tour of the brewery grounds, he notes that the buildings sided with white brick are original; the others have been added on during a succession of expansions. The biggest was in 1985, when the addition of a second brew house doubled capacity to eight million barrels. In 2011, the company completed a $34 million facilities upgrade that boosted capacity to its current rate, from twelve million barrels annually, and made the plant more efficient with its water usage. It claims to be the biggest customer of the city's water system.

The company also spent $40 million to overhaul its nearby Longhorn Glass plant, where it forges 2.2 million of the amber twelve-ounce bottles

Massive lagering tanks at the Anheuser-Busch InBev Houston plant, which produces 12.5 million barrels of Bud Light, ZiegenBock and other beers each year. *Photo by Ronnie Crocker.*

embossed with that eagle logo every day. Like the brewery's production line, the bottle factory in full swing is a mesmerizing sight: molten glass, glowing bright red at temperatures up to 2,800 degrees, oozes from a furnace through a series of insulated lines toward two forming lines. In a four-second flash, the bottles are molded into shape and turned over two at a time on their way to an annealing oven, where they are slowly cooled to prevent breakage.

But Anheuser-Busch is always looking for ways to wring more from the plant because its target Texas market, in company parlance, is "oversold." It takes fifteen million barrels' worth of beer to meet current demand, and beer has to be shipped in from Anheuser-Busch's eleven other U.S. breweries to cover the gap.

The next expansion is already underway, a $30 million project to open a new packaging line dedicated to the increasingly popular twenty-four-ounce aluminum cans. These double-size beers currently share time on a line with ten-ounce cans sold primarily in Puerto Rico. Dedicating a line for the big cans is expected to boost production by another million barrels come 2013.

"Twenty-four-ounce cans, twenty-four hours a day, seven days a week," Maxwell says with a grin, "just to keep Texans happy."

It's hard to imagine Bud Light going the way of Grand Prize or Southern Select, and the multimillion-dollar upgrades suggest a secure future for the Houston brewery—good news for local labor. But not all Texans are happy with the company's corporate behavior these days. During the summer of 2011, a vocal minority grew downright hostile, particularly on social media, after lobbying by Anheuser-Busch sank a bill designed to help the state's small craft breweries by letting people take home a small amount of their beer after brewery tours. This lobbying effort came twenty-one years after the company had secured special treatment for itself from the legislature in a deal derided as the "sea mammal exclusion," which excepted it from the same prohibition on manufacturers' selling directly to the public after its purchase of the Sea World amusement parks.

The company sought that exemption because its purchase included the Sea World park in San Antonio, and state law technically forbade it from putting its own beer on tap there. In the manner of the way these things are handled in Texas, the carefully crafted law change allowed brewers who keep sea mammals in a marine park on 250 acres, give or take 5 acres, in a county whose population exceeded 950,000 to go ahead and sell beer there. The wording meant the exemption applied to just one place: Sea World, in San Antonio, the county seat of Bexar County.

But in 2011, the company fought a bill with similarly constrained wording that would allow brewers that manufactured fewer than 75,000 barrels annually not to sell beer directly to customers but to let them take home one or two souvenir six-packs following brewery tours. The amount of beer these tourists could walk out with varied, depending on how much they'd paid for the tour.

Supporters of the bill said it would help new and smaller breweries with marketing. Anheuser-Busch, which hasn't hosted public tours of its Houston plant for years, argued that it was unfair to not include the bigger breweries. Two years earlier, when the bill was introduced without that exception, it was quietly killed in a committee.

Spurred by the setback, a couple of restaurants announced boycotts of Anheuser-Busch products, and a group of frustrated beer aficionados formed a consumer lobby called Open the Taps to advocate for changes to

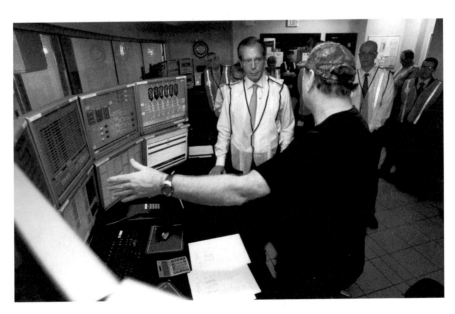

Texas lieutenant governor David Dewhurst got a tour of the Anheuser-Busch InBev Houston plant in the wake of the company's latest multimillion-dollar upgrade. *Photo by Brett Coomer*/Houston Chronicle.

the state's alcohol laws that would encourage competition from within and from outside Texas.

Not everything had gone so much in Anheuser-Busch's favor. Three years earlier, the descendants of Adolphus Busch lost control of the company, and the most iconic of American brands had ceased to be American owned.

The first decade of the twenty-first century found the domestic brewing industry in yet another period of upheaval. As the overall beer market stagnated, smaller, independently owned craft breweries grew in number and in popularity. Even if their customer base remained tiny compared with their mass-market competitors, these new breweries—along with wineries and spirits producers—were steadily draining away drinkers from the big-three brand families of Bud, Miller and Coors (BMC). Even through a stubborn economic malaise, craft-beer sales continued to soar, and hundreds of microbreweries and brewpubs opened nationwide. They offered an unprecedented array of flavorful ales, wheats, stouts, porters and more. Though they cost more than the BMC alternatives, craft beers were effectively marketed as an "affordable luxury."

Consolidation at the top was inevitable, as the brewers looked to cut costs and operate more efficiently, but this time it would have an international flavor. South African Breweries took over Miller Brewing in 2002, and Canada's Molson merged with Adolph Coors in 2005. The combined companies, SABMiller and Molson Coors, subsequently formed a joint venture, MillerCoors, for their U.S. operations.

The biggest shakeup came in 2008 when Anheuser-Busch, under the leadership of Adolphus Busch's great-great-grandson August A. Busch IV, was swallowed up by the aggressive, bottom-line-oriented brewing giant InBev. The Belgium-based conglomerate, rooted in Brazil, itself was the result of a global merger in 2004. The $52 billion deal made Budweiser InBev's leading brand worldwide, alongside Stella Artois and Beck's, but it downgraded St. Louis's status to North American regional headquarters.

Rumors of an Anheuser-Busch InBev-SABMiller alliance soon followed, although it seemed unlikely that regulators in the United States would allow a single conglomerate to control more than three-quarters of the nation's beer market.

At the close of 2011, Anheuser-Busch InBev maintained a dominant 48.3 percent share, but that was down from its high of 52 percent, and its financial report for the year's third quarter reflected weakness in the U.S. market that may prove to be more than a function of the economic funk. While Budweiser volumes increased 6.9 percent worldwide over the three-month period, that was due to growth in China and other international markets, including a launch in Brazil. Budweiser numbers fell in the United States, and the company reported it was "very pleased" to merely have slowed its decline in market share. Anheuser-Busch InBev said it would continue to focus on Bud Light, citing a new NFL sponsorship and the impending release of a higher-alcohol product called Bud Light Platinum in time for the 2012 Super Bowl.

The Houston brewery's general manager, Rick Wohlfarth, acknowledged there had been layoffs in 2010, but he said the following spring that the plant was hiring again. "From our perspective in Texas," he said, "we're in a growing industry." Maxwell said much the same thing in December: "Sales in Texas are going up every day."

Maxwell and Cohen say the InBev takeover has not dramatically affected their working lives. In fact, they say they see a real and practical benefit to owning breweries in places like China and Europe, where Anheuser-Busch once had to depend on licensees to brew its beer. It gives the company, and its brewers, more control over production.

For John Nau III, president of Silver Eagle Distributors, another major Houston employer and the nation's largest Anheuser-Busch wholesaler, the post-merger changes have been fairly prosaic. For example, Silver Eagle for years had picked up its orders directly from the local brewery, which is just a few miles away. But Anheuser-Busch InBev prefers to handle all freight leaving its myriad plants, and in early November, it started using its own fleet to deliver beer to the Silver Eagle warehouses. Nau says none of his drivers had to be laid off because of the change, and the excess trucks were either redeployed within the fleet or sold.

Nau says his meetings with Anheuser-Busch InBev management have been positive, and Silver Eagle deals with the same field force from the brewery. Still, Nau recalls being taken aback at news of the merger. His initial concern, he says, was whether the global firm would maintain a strong commitment to the Anheuser-Busch line. Three years in, based on his own interactions and the capital investments he's seen the parent company make in Houston and elsewhere, he's convinced InBev is a "brand builder."

A massive fleet of trucks is required to deliver Bud Light, ZiegenBock and other Anheuser-Busch InBev products made in Houston. *Photo courtesy of Silver Eagle Distributors.*

But Nau and other local distributors are rapidly responding to other changing conditions that have put pressure on the major producers. Silver Eagle's acquisition of the Glazer Family of Companies, completed in January 2009, added the local Saint Arnold Brewing Company and more than seventy other craft brands to its portfolio. Nau takes personal credit for some of the subsequent additions. He went after Big Sky Brewing after trying a Moose Drool brown ale on a hunting trip in Wyoming, he says, and got to know Stevens Point Brewery during fishing trips to Wisconsin.

Nau says these and other craft beers have boosted Silver Eagle's market share by two and a half to three points, to a commanding 68 percent in its local territory. At Houston Distributing Company (HDC), which not many years ago was exclusively a Miller wholesaler, craft beers now make up 14 percent of its business and imports make up 24 percent. In the fall of 2011, Vice-President Scotty Heckel put together the first HDC Brew Fest, a coming-out party of sorts to personally acquaint retailers and bar industry representatives with these growing lines. In Galveston and Beaumont, where the one-hundred-year-old Del Papa Distributing handles the Bud brands, the Del Papa marketing staff has begun hosting free public tastings each month to introduce people to its craft brands. Meanwhile, smaller distributors like

Duff Beer Distribution have carved out a lucrative niche handling non-BMC crafts and imports. A trip down any grocery store beer aisle confirms that Houstonians have more choices than ever.

Meanwhile, the number of craft breweries operating in Houston has swelled to five, with another beer company and a hard-cider company selling their own brands that are produced elsewhere on contract; more groups are openly discussing plans to open breweries. Before 2008, Saint Arnold had this segment to itself, but so far all seem to be benefiting from the increased consumer attention.

The beer boom in Houston is back! And this time it'll last, right?

Chapter 7

Home-Brewers and the Brief, Glorious Brewpub Era

The United States counted 766 breweries in operation in 1935, the year domestic brewing began a long period of consolidation that lasted more than four decades. Production more than doubled during this period, but fewer and fewer companies were making the beer. At its 1979 low point, there were just 44 U.S. breweries, and 2 of those were in the Beer Institute's relatively new "specialty" category. The number of "traditional" breweries, which made the national brands available to the vast majority of Americans, continued to drop, and by 2006 there were only 20 of these. The number of wholesalers experienced a similar contraction. Meanwhile, aggressive advertising campaigns promoting light lagers made with adjuncts such as rice further restricted the amount of choice in bars and stores.

As the Brewers Association, a trade group for craft breweries, puts it: "Up until the early-1980s, the popular image of beer in America was simply that of a mass-produced commodity with little or no character, tradition or culture worth mentioning."

In this environment, competition at the top grew increasingly fierce, and by the early 1990s, a business professor at the College of William and Mary was explaining to his graduate class that, since brewing was a mature industry and all beer tasted pretty much the same, the beer companies had to rely on marketing to steal customers from each other. The MBA students, who'd grown up watching "Tastes great! Less filling!" television commercials for Miller Lite, offered no argument.

A Heady History of Brewing in the Bayou City

But changes were stirring at an individual level, across the country, in the nation's garages, driveways and backyards. Just as they had during Prohibition, Americans in the 1970s and 1980s who wanted beer they couldn't get at the store started brewing it themselves. Men like Charlie Papazian, co-founder in 1978 of the American Homebrewers Association and author in 1984 of *The Complete Joy of Homebrewing*, helped coalesce these shade-tree brewers into an active movement, from which many of the early microbreweries and brewpubs directly sprang. Today, it is rare to meet a professional craft brewer who doesn't have at least some do-it-yourself background.

Houston developed a thriving home-brewing scene that has endured over three decades. A dedicated core of home-brewers helped shape the area's modern beer culture in often profound ways well into the twenty-first century. Consumers who take for granted the variety of brands and styles now available on the beer aisle owe these guys a round. They made beer for themselves, and some of them made beer for a living, at least for a time. They promoted good beer and supported the new pioneers who started making local beer in the 1990s, even if the broader public wasn't ready yet to sustain them. The longtime epicenter of this movement is DeFalco's Home Wine and Beer Supplies and its owner, Scott Birdwell, a skilled brewer, teacher and businessman, a nationally certified master beer judge and a mentor to many fine amateur brewers. He got interested the way many people of his generation did, through overseas travel.

A three-month, fifteen-country tour of Europe in 1977 opened Birdwell's eyes to the possibilities for just how good beer could be, and he came home with a refined palate and a determination to make beer that would satisfy it. "Everywhere I went, the beer was better than in the United States," he told a *Chronicle* interviewer in 1998 at the beginning of his two-and-a-half-year run as the newspaper's beer columnist. "When I was in Europe, I saw home-brewers' supplies in the windows, and that sort of planted the seeds that you could make this stuff at home."

Birdwell brewed his first batch in January 1978, several months before Congress and President Jimmy Carter cleared the way for states to legalize home-brewing. He began working at DeFalco's, and although the ban on home-brewing was not actively enforced, he recalls, "It's very difficult to promote a hobby that is technically against the law." Birdwell bought DeFalco's in 1980, and three years later he helped get a bill to legalize home-brewing before the Texas Legislature. The measure passed, with "no organized opposition," and Governor Mark White signed it into law.

Texas had officially joined the craft-beer revolution, even if most Texans wouldn't realize it for several years.

Boiling hops during a Foam Rangers brew-in at DeFalco's Home Wine and Beer Supplies shop, fall 2011. *Photo by Ronnie Crocker.*

In 1981, Birdwell helped found the Foam Rangers, and he still hosts meetings and monthly "brew-ins" at his supply shop, which, after a series of moves, recently settled into a seven-thousand-square-foot space inside the city's Inner Loop. After the state law change of 1983, the Foam Rangers organized a citywide home-brewing competition and the following year sponsored the first Dixie Cup. It quickly became one of the nation's largest regional competitions for home-brewers, and for a stretch in the mid-2000s, it was the largest single-site competition in the world. Featured speakers have included such craft-beer luminaries as Brooklyn Brewing's Garrett Oliver, author of *The Brewmaster's Table*; former Anchor Brewing owner Fritz Maytag; and the late Pierre Celis, the Belgian-born founder of Hoegaarden and, in 1992, the Celis microbrewery in the Texas Hill Country. Legendary beer writer Fred Eckhardt was a frequent Dixie Cup guest, and his image is still incorporated into many themed T-shirts. The twenty-eighth competition, in October 2011, drew more than one thousand entries representing more than a dozen clubs, including a few from outside Texas.

Yet, like the professional brewing industry, the home-brewing hobby is proving to be cyclical. The pastime boomed in the early 1990s, when Birdwell recalls seeing brew-it-yourself kits popping up in such mainstream outlets as Bed, Bath and Beyond. That was followed by a bust around 1996, when, he says, "the bottom fell out." Part of that contraction may have been tied to the strong economy and the fact that people had more money than free time, he says, but part of it, too, was a positive change in the beer environment. "Suddenly," Birdwell says, "you no longer had to make it yourself if you wanted something good. You could just go out and buy it." He was part of a group that drew up a business plan to open a local craft brewery. That effort stalled, but DeFalco's persevered to benefit from another boom that began in the late 2000s. Birdwell's shop draws quite a crowd on Saturday mornings, and his introductory beer-making classes routinely sell out. In 2011, he reports, sales were up around 15 percent over the year before.

Scott Birdwell is the dean of Houston home-brewers. This is him in 1979, the year after Congress legalized home-brewing in America. *Photo by Carlos Antonio Rios/*Houston Chronicle.

The serious home-brewers never went away. As one says, they'd all drunk the same Kool-Aid. In 1997, a local-access television program called *The Malt Show* began highlighting the enthusiasm, energy and expertise they bring to their craft.

In an early episode, host Bev D. Blackwood II takes viewers along as three members of the Foam Rangers conduct a backyard experiment, making the same bock beer recipe with three distinctly different processes. A basic infusion system common among home-brewers serves as the control in a friendly competition against a more labor-intensive decoction method, in which parts of the mash are ladled out, boiled separately and added back to raise the temperature of the mash, and a comparatively more sophisticated recirculating infusion mash system, or RIMS. At stake were mere bragging rights, but the brewers took the challenge seriously. The owner of this particular RIMS system, an attorney named Louis Bonham, had tricked out his equipment to give it a bit more firepower. Later in the episode, Bonham opens the door to a small closet in his house that he had converted into a laboratory, complete with a pH meter, one-thousand-power microscope, an ultraviolet spectrometer to calculate the color and bitterness of beer samples and a grain scale to measure the salt content of water. There is a cushioned stool to sit on and a small library of home-brewing manuals and guides. A glass jug contains a preparation of yeast that soon would be added to ferment the beer.

Frantz Brogniez and Charles Lieberman would've approved.

Yet for all the care and scientific precision that goes into home-brewing, the hobby is an inherently social one. Its allure will always be more than calculating original and final gravities. As Blackwood noted in summing up the segment on the bock experiment, "Of course, no matter what the outcome, there is always a cold beer at the end of it."

That sense of humor would be tested soon enough.

Birdwell and others were lobbying the state legislature again in the early 1990s, this time to make it legal for a restaurant or bar to brew beer on the premises and sell it to customers directly. By the 1993 session, they'd built enough momentum to get the bill through—and launch another beer boom.

A Heady History of Brewing in the Bayou City

The Village Brewery, shown here under construction in 1994, was built to showcase the beers made on site. *Photo by John Everett/*Houston Chronicle.

For the next several years, brewpubs were all the rage. "It seemed like there was a new place opening up every week and a half," says Blackwood, whose *Malt Show* archives are about all that's left of any of them. By the time the fad passed, at least eighteen brewpubs had come and gone in the Houston-Galveston area. They are fondly recalled today.

"It was a fun job to have when you're a kid," recalls Max Miyamoto, who worked his way up from bartender to head brewer at the city's first brewpub and went on to win national accolades for his work. In the race to open before their competitors, the owners of the Village Brewery invested upward of $4 million to convert a former post office building near the Rice University campus (and just a few blocks from Birdwell's shop at the time) into a handsome restaurant with hardwood floors, an open kitchen and gleaming copper tanks. They kicked off the brewpub era in April 1994 with such beers as Houston Wheat, Village Pale Ale, Amber Owl Ale (a nod to the Rice sports mascot) and Armadillo Stout.

To showcase the brewing system, designers placed a ten-barrel brew house in one corner of the restaurant and five fermentation tanks in another corner, with ten serving tanks opposite from them. "They really cared about how it looked," says Miyamoto.

As demonstrated decades before by the old Grand Prize tours, the spectacle of letting customers see where their beer is made—with the added bonus of drinking it fresh from the tanks—has a strong appeal. Beer tourism was back.

"You are kind of on stage," brewer Tim Case of the acclaimed Houston Brewery, one of two brewpubs to open in 1994 on the then-hot nightlife strip along Richmond Avenue, explained to Blackwood on *The Malt Show*. "I think that's kind of necessary for a brewpub. People get a big kick out of seeing the beer being brewed right there." But these were strange brews to most Houstonians, and customers needed a friendly guide through the uncertain terrain of bitters and steams, helles bocks and Oktoberfests. On Saturdays, Case invited customers into the brew house for free tours. Miyamoto recalls that the Village Brewery bar staff was trained to be prepared for questions as well.

"I enjoyed teaching people about it," he says. "I enjoyed making it. And I sure enjoyed drinking it."

Miyamoto was twenty-three years old when he started tending bar there, fresh from the University of Houston but already well acquainted with the restaurant business. In college, he'd gotten hooked on imports and the emerging craft beers at the Ginger Man, a Rice Village fixture since 1985 and one of the few places in town that served them. He started with Bass and Guinness. "All of a sudden," he adds, "I wanted to try all of them." He was working at the Village Brewery during the Houston Rockets' electrifying second straight NBA championship run in 1995. "The whole Village was really crazy then," he says.

The decorative design of the brewery made it labor-intensive, too, and Miyamoto's job included cleaning the long lines the beer had to travel from one phase of production to the next. He would come in during the day to scrub tanks and spray down the fermenters. He learned how to read sugar levels of fermenting beer during daily checks with a hydrometer. He took up home-brewing on the side—keeping two or three kegs going at home made him popular with his roommates—and did a lot of independent reading. After a year and a half as an assistant brewer, Miyamoto got the opportunity to move up. When his predecessor left for a job in Pittsburgh, the owners brought in an experienced professional brewer with a background in microbiology to train Miyamoto to take over the top job.

For the next three and a half years, he made beer full time and was an active member of the Houston Craft Brewers Guild. The brewers may have been competitors, but they were always willing to help each other out.

"They would work together, which was nice," says Blackwood, who also wrote about the guild for the *Southwest Brewing News* and recalls brewers sharing equipment, ingredients and expertise. "We used to piggyback on grain orders," adds Miyamoto. "If someone had a problem, everyone would throw in their two cents' worth." They organized festivals downtown to publicize their restaurants and raise money for lobbying efforts.

Miyamoto also visited local home-brew clubs, not only the Foam Rangers but also the Bay Area Mashtronauts in the Clear Lake area and the Kuykendahl Gran Brewers (KGB) based in north Houston. There, he promoted his brewpub, helped judge competitions, made friends and drank beer. "I used to say it was marketing, but I was just having a good time." Meanwhile, he was also refining his craft, and in 1997, one of his beers, an English-style strong ale, won a gold medal at the Great American Beer Festival.

Blackwood recalls that the home-brewers were supportive of the brewpubs in return, organizing monthly outings as they opened up from Galveston and the Clear Lake area to Houston's northern and western outskirts. In fact, many of the brewers were also members of the Foam Rangers. Case, of the Houston Brewery, was tenured in the bar business and started home-

Max Miyamoto is a veteran of Houston's brewpub heyday. In 1997, he won a gold medal at the Great American Beer Festival for one of his brews, an English-style strong ale. *Photo by Ronnie Crocker.*

brewing in 1986 after serving as a judge for several of the early Dixie Cup competitions. "As a friend of mine said, I used to have a great hobby. Now, I've got a job," he told *The Malt Show.*

This period was heavenly for Houston home-brewers. The more ambitious ones seized the opportunity to turn their hobby into a job; everyone else was just happy to find fresh beer that they liked to drink. "Everybody was driven to make better beer," says Blackwood. The pubs and the brewers were diverse and interesting. At one point, the Rice Village was home to three brewpubs, including Miyamoto's place, the cozy Bank Draft and the restaurant-first Two Rows. The national chain Rock Bottom staked a claim on Richmond Avenue, not far from the Houston Brewery. While retrofitting a building for a new downtown brewpub called the Mercantile, the owners uncovered the ornamental relics of an old movie theater and left them as part of the décor. There was a waterfront place in Seabrook and two more brewpubs in Galveston. A now-deceased brewer in Clear Lake loved to make lagers and talk beer with the German engineers who worked at NASA; he later opened a pair of brewpubs in Shanghai, China. "He was something else," recalls Blackwood. "He just had that huge spirit that you expect a lot of Texas people to have." Another brewer had been an oilfield welder and made many of the home-brewing systems that are still being used around town. Once, at a party at his house in the southwestern suburb of Richmond, guests were required to try their hand at welding.

"It was a fun time," says Blackwood. "It was hard for anybody to see how that could go wrong. Everybody seemed to be doing OK."

But one by one, for varying reasons, the brewpubs started closing. For some, the overhead proved to be too much. Others struggled once the initial excitement wore off or the neighborhoods they'd built in became less trendy. Houston can be tough on restaurants to begin with, and no doubt some operators were simply better at making beer than making money.

"I would endeavor to say no single brewpub in Houston went out of business because they made bad beer," says Blackwood. "Some of them made average beer, but none of them made bad beer."

By the end of the decade, only one of the local brewpubs that opened in the 1990s was still making beer. Three others remain open as bars or restaurants, but they long ago stopped brewing their own beer. Miyamoto was one of the last to give it a try. After the Village Brewery changed to a swing-dance/supper club concept for a short period, then closed for good in 1998, Miyamoto worked other restaurant jobs and then opened the chain-owned Hofbrau Steaks and Brewery on the northwest side. It didn't last, and in September 2003, he and a

For a brief period, the Bank Draft was one of three brewpubs operating in Rice Village alone. By the end of the 1990s, the brewpub era was all but done. *Photo by D. Fahleson/* Houston Chronicle.

business partner opened Side Street Brewing with equipment from the old Bay Brewery in Seabrook. Heeding the lessons of all those predecessors, they opted for a small space and minimal staff to reduce overhead. Miyamoto did triple duty as manager, brewer and chef, and he says they came close to making a profit. But still they ran out of money after just a few months and shuttered the place. Houston's last survivor, Two Rows, part of a North Texas–based chain that focused on the restaurant side of the business, closed in 2010.

The nation's fourth-largest city was officially bereft of brewpubs, but the brewpub era had essentially been over for years.

"Your reaction was like, 'Man,'" says Blackwood. It took a while to understand what happened. The true enthusiasts may have drunk the craft beer Kool-Aid, but to a large extent Houston was still a Bud town. "The availability of better beer doesn't mean everybody is going to drink it," Blackwood says. Many of the brewers, like Case, moved out of the area.

"I think a lot of them felt like they got burned by the business," Blackwood says. "They went into it with a lot of hope."

Miyamoto turned to professional poker, traveling a circuit and playing in major tournaments from Mississippi to California. For the last six years, he's participated in the World Series of Poker in Las Vegas and has made it as far as the fourth table. But at age forty, he says, the lifestyle is starting to feel more like a grind than a grand adventure. He's thinking about trying a brewpub once again, though his plans are so preliminary he's not ready to discuss them. Side Street, he says, came tantalizingly close to success, and he thinks Houston is a more beer-savvy market these days. If craft beer is less exotic now, it's less intimidating, too—and more popular than ever. Miyamoto is confident in his business smarts as well as his brewing skills: "I think today if you were going to do one, you'd need someone like me who can do everything, so your overhead isn't so high."

He seems wistful for the days when he was a wildcatter of ale, striking gold with Houston brew.

"It wasn't that long ago," he says, "but it seems like a long time ago."

Many great brewers never draw a paycheck for their work. They excel in their hobby but never decide to go professional. In Houston, two of the most successful amateurs bring to their craft Brogniez- or Lieberman-worthy backgrounds. One is a chemical engineer, and the other is living proof that, while you may not need to be a rocket scientist to brew great beer, it sure doesn't hurt.

Foam Ranger Mike Heniff earned the affectionate nickname "Beeriac" for his maniacal devotion to studying and making quality beer. The garage of his suburban home in Pearland is well equipped for the hobby, and in his personal study the walls are festooned with colorful ribbons he's earned over the course of his "home-brewing career." A bookshelf is lined with heavy statues recognizing the major awards. A side table is weighted down by several wood-and-glass frames that he's yet to hang. Each is filled with bottle caps from beers he's had over the years, many of them arranged by region and/or style.

Hiawatha beer was advertised by Houston Ice and
Brewing Company as "absolutely non-intoxicating."
Collection of Bob Kay, bobkaybeerlabels.com.

The American Brewing Association was built in Houston in the 1890s by none other than
Adolphus Busch. *Collection of Bob Kay, bobkaybeerlabels.com.*

Commemorative tin for Hiawatha, an early Houston beer. *Collection of Philip Brogniez.*

Top: Brass tap handles for Southern Select and Magnolia, two early beers brewed first in Houston and, after Prohibition, in Galveston. *Collection of Ralph W. Stenzel Jr. Photographed by Ronnie Crocker.*

Bottom: John Jurgensen was in Mission Control during the first lunar landing and retired from NASA in 2009. He's also an award-winning home-brewer. *Photo by Julio Cortez/*Houston Chronicle.

The Bay Area Mashtronauts dubbed their annual home-brew competition Lunar Rendezbrew. The eighteenth annual event was held in 2011. *Courtesy of the Bay Area Mashtronauts.*

After winning a home-brew competition, Phillip Kaufman of the Kuykendahl Gran Brewers was invited to help brew his Scotch ale at Saint Arnold Brewing Company in 2009. It was released as Divine Reserve No. 8. *Photo by Julio Cortez/*Houston Chronicle.

Brewmaster Tim Case of the acclaimed Houston Brewery in 1998, toward the end of the city's brewpub era. *Photo by Karen Warren/*Houston Chronicle.

The Houston Brewery, as it was in 1999. *Photo by John Everett/*Houston Chronicle.

The Mercantile, in an old nickelodeon theater, was a short-lived brewpub in downtown Houston. *Photo by John Everett/*Houston Chronicle.

The Brews Brothers opened on The Strand in Galveston in 2011. The owners made a beer aged in oak from trees felled during 2008's Hurricane Ike and hope to begin selling their own beers on-site once they get brewing equipment in place. *Photo by Ronnie Crocker.*

Brock Wagner and others from the Saint Arnold crew await the judges' results during the 2011 Great American Beer Festival. The Houston brewery had taken two gold and two silver medals over the previous two years, but Wagner and company went home empty-handed this time. *Photo by Ronnie Crocker.*

Saint Arnold's new fall 2011 seasonal, Pumpkinator, debuted as Divine Reserve No. 9 in 2009. *Photo by Ronnie Crocker.*

Saint Arnold's limited-release Divine Reserve series beers had always been popular, but by 2009 they were selling out in minutes. *Photo by Brett Coomer/Houston Chronicle.*

This Bentley became the first of the tie-dyed Saint Arnold cars. *Photo by E. Joseph Deering/* Houston Chronicle.

Bev D. Blackwood II, a home-brewer, beer writer and one-time professional brewer, dressed up as Saint Arnold in 2002. *Photo by D. Fahleson/*Houston Chronicle.

From left: Dave Fougeron of Southern Star Brewing Company, Brock Wagner of Saint Arnold and Eric Warner of Karbach are at the center of the Houston area's craft-beer scene. *Photo by Ronnie Crocker.*

Southern Star's delicious Buried Hatchet Stout is potent enough that a four-pack is more than enough. *Photo by Brett Coomer/Houston Chronicle.*

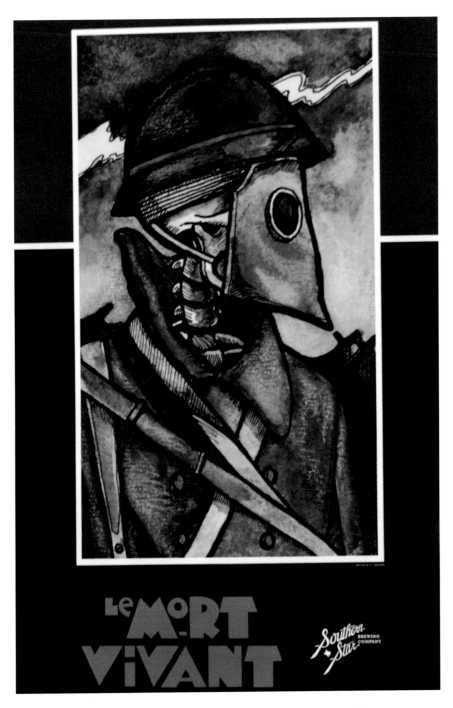

Local artist Michael Draper provided the distinctive artwork for Le Mort Vivant, a Southern Star seasonal. Draper's work is featured on all of the Conroe brewery's cans. *Photo by Ronnie Crocker.*

Jennifer and Brian Royo opened No Label Brewing Company in an old rice dryer in Katy. *Photo by Billy Smith II/*Houston Chronicle.

From left: Chris Fall, Eric Warner, David Greenwood and David Graham toast the imminent opening of Karbach Brewing Company, the Houston area's fourth craft brewery. *Photo by Ronnie Crocker.*

Houston's brand-new Karbach Brewing Company released Sympathy for the Lager to a lot of local buzz. *Photo by Johnny Hanson/*Houston Chronicle.

The full Karbach crew celebrates the brewery's first night in the market at Liberty Station, in September 2011. *Photo by Ronnie Crocker.*

Traveling Texans: A demonstrative group of Houstonians showed up in Denver for the 2011 Great American Beer Festival. *Photo by Ronnie Crocker.*

With a state license in hand, the crew of 8th Wonder Brewing Company—named for the Houston Astrodome—are planning on a spring 2012 opening that would make it the area's sixth craft brewery. *From left:* Matt Marcus, Aaron Corsi, Alex Vassilakidis and Ryan Soroka. *Photo by James Nielsen/* Houston Chronicle.

These Houstonians were part of a group that traveled to New Orleans to taste several Cantillon lambics for Zwanze Day. Against the wall is Saint Arnold brewer Aaron Inkrott. Seated are Serah and Brian Ingram. *Photo by Ronnie Crocker.*

The venerable Ginger Man pub was an early supporter of craft beer in Houston. General manager Joe Jackson put on a twenty-fifth anniversary party in 2010. *Photo by Julio Cortez/* Houston Chronicle.

Scott Birdwell was home-brewing in Houston before it was technically legal. His DeFalco's Home Wine and Beer Supplies shop plays host to Foam Rangers meetings and monthly brew-ins. *Photo by Julio Cortez/*Houston Chronicle.

A Heady History of Brewing in the Bayou City

As the brewpub era was kicking off in Houston, Heniff was working on a chemical-engineering degree at the University of Illinois, and his palate was graduating from typical college-fare suds to the likes of Guinness, Pete's Wicked Lager and Celis White. Eager to learn more about craft beers, Heniff turned to UseNet, an early iteration of Internet forums, to see what other fans were saying. This launched a lifetime of meticulous study, and over the next seventeen years, he compiled a running inventory of detailed tasting notes for the different commercial beers he'd tried. Originally, he says, he started maintaining the list to keep track of which beers he didn't like, so he wouldn't waste money ordering them again. He was moved to start the list when he accidentally ordered a second "ghastly" Pete's Wicked Winter Brew. As of early 2012, the list is maintained in an Excel spreadsheet and includes more than 3,800 entries.

With a copy of Papazian's *New Complete Joy of Homebrewing* in hand, Heniff made his first and second attempts at home-brewing in Morris, Illinois, while working for a chemical company as part of his college program. The first was an American pale ale made with a liquid malt extract and a packet of dry yeast that came with it. The second was an American brown ale into which he steeped grains along with a liquid extract. Both flopped, and before he would attempt another batch, he was married, living in Houston and employed at one of the area's many chemical plants. Apartment life had

Foam Ranger Mike Heniff is one of the Houston area's most accomplished home-brewers. His home in the suburb of Pearland features many of his awards. *Photo by Ronnie Crocker.*

meant home-brewing wasn't feasible, and his job in the lucrative chemical industry meant he could easily afford the craft beers he enjoyed. But he drove past a home-brew supply shop on his way to work and back each day, "a constant reminder" of the challenge he'd yet to conquer. By 1997, Heniff and his wife were in a house, and he bought some new equipment and a pale ale kit for another attempt. This time, the malt extract was old. "Again, stalled fermentation," says Heniff.

Finally, he made a porter that hinted at his talents as a home-brewer. He also discovered another home-brew shop, where he felt he was getting better advice. On May 21, 1998, he asked for a recipe for a beer that tasted like Duvel. The shop owner wrote it down off the top of his head. The beer used liquid yeast and turned out to be "far and away" better than any of his first four. Heniff was hooked on his new hobby and humbled by the expertise he'd seen in action.

"That guy behind the counter was none other than Scott Birdwell," he says. "It just blew me away that someone could know that much about beer."

Nearly a decade earlier, in 1989, Birdwell had become just the fifth person in the United States deemed a master by the American Homebrewers Association's Beer Judge Certification Program. It's a distinction attained only with superior scores on a judging exam and extensive experience judging beer competitions. Suggesting how dauntingly difficult it can be to reach this rank, the AHA didn't reach one hundred masters until December 2011. By then, Texas could claim three, all of them Foam Rangers. Birdwell and Heniff had earned the even rarer title of grand master.

Heniff would distinguish himself making beer as well as judging it. His first competition entry was batch No. 28—Heniff keeps records of his home-brews that are as detailed as his tasting notes—a Belgian dubbel that scored well in the 2000 Dixie Cup but didn't medal. His first medal was for a second-place finish at the 2001 Bluebonnet competition in Dallas. The beer was an India pale ale, and the silver medal supercharged Heniff's competitive instincts. "I began brewing at a more rapid pace," he says; through 2008, he estimates he brewed about eighteen times a year and collected roughly two hundred medals and other awards. Oddly, considering his otherwise obsessive record keeping, he says, "I don't have an exact count."

The temptation to turn pro was strong, and Heniff says he struggled with the decision. Chemical engineering pays well; brewing, not so much. Besides, he still had a passion for engineering, not to mention a family. Ultimately, home-brewing, like judging, was something he did on the side, strictly for personal fulfillment. "The same thing happens for people who write poetry, paint paintings, act in plays," he says.

But a half-dozen or so of his beers have been brewed commercially. The most notable one of these came in 2007, when he won the KGB-sponsored Big Batch Brew Bash, a competitive single-style brew-off in which he entered two Russian imperial stouts made with similar recipes. The first came from Heniff's personal batch No. 113, which by then had been aging for more than a year, and the more recent vintage No. 130, from only three or four months earlier. When the winners were announced, Heniff's beers had finished first and second, respectively. Late that August, Houston's original craft brewery, Saint Arnold Brewing Company, released the beer as part of its esteemed Divine Reserve series.

Just 1,276 cases of the beer, Divine Reserve No. 5, were made, with a deceptively high alcohol content of 10 percent by volume. Today, on the beer-rating boards at BeerAdvocate.com, Heniff's beer merits a "world-class" 96; RateBeer.com scores it even higher, at a 99. Even Heniff, a man who chooses his words as carefully as he puts his beers together, acknowledges that DR5 was "extremely well received." But unlike some Brew Bash winners who come in as "brewer for a day," Heniff was content to let the Saint Arnold staff handle the commercial manufacture without him.

Likewise, John Jurgensen has wondered off and on if he could make it as a professional brewer. "I think all of us dream of that," he says.

Then again, a lot of Americans dream about Jurgensen's career: rocket scientist. He was one of NASA's whiz kids of manned spaceflight, on duty at Mission Control when the astronauts aboard Apollo 11 made the first-ever lunar landing in 1969. He was twenty-four when the words came down from the moon: "Houston, Tranquility Base here. The Eagle has landed."

Jurgensen had come to NASA, and to Clear Lake, in 1967. Before that, he was at Indiana University studying mathematics and drinking the "cheap swill" that is *de rigueur* for college students. He'd been a baker's assistant for a short spell and knew that he loved working with yeast, but it would be more than two decades before he tried his hand at making beer. That seed was planted, however, during a trip to DeFalco's to buy a bottle-capper for an antique Coca-Cola machine his wife had bought. "I walked in there and said, 'Oh, they have everything you need to make your own beer.' That sat in my brain." The notion germinated until the spring of 1994, when the Jurgensens moved to a larger house in a suburb closer to Houston. By the time he started brewing, Jurgensen was fifty years old. In addition to his history-making work with the space program, he taught college math at

Best-in-Show stein from Lunar Rendezbrew XVIII. The annual competition is sponsored by the Bay Area Mashtronauts. *Photo by Ronnie Crocker.*

the University of Houston–Downtown, and he has coauthored a geometry textbook that is still used in high schools.

Beer was another problem to solve.

"Every batch I made got consistently worse," he recalls. Then he joined the Bay Area Mashtronauts and was paired with a more experienced brewer, Joachim Beek, a software developer in the space industry, for his first Nuts and Bolts club competition. "That's when I learned how to make good beer," says Jurgensen. He progressed quickly and won his first American

A Heady History of Brewing in the Bayou City

Homebrewers Association medal in 2004, taking first place from among 110 entries nationally in the spice/herb/vegetable beer category with an American wheat with honey that he brewed and infused with a tincture of jalapeño-soaked vodka and then entered as a pepper beer. To get the flavor he wanted, Jurgensen added drops of the solution from an eyedropper into a twelve-ounce glass.

Jurgensen further honed his brewing skills with fellow Mashtronaut Jeff Oberlin. He soon was making excellent ciders and meads, and in 2006, he was named the AHA's Cidermaker of the Year. He has amassed upward of one hundred more medals in the years since and is a regular feature at the Mashtronauts' answer to the Dixie Cup: the annual Lunar Rendezbrew.

No brewer, he says, can excel without the tutelage of others. He started by reading. "I learned how to make beer," he says. "From Joachim, I learned how to make good beer. From Jeff Oberlin, I learned how to make very good beer." And he is passing on his skills as well. He taught Oberlin's wife, Cindy, how to make cider, and he is proud to note that she has gone on to beat him in competition.

After retiring from NASA in 2009, Jurgensen and his wife moved to San Antonio. He converted a garage bay into a brewing room and pub, with two fermenting tanks, an eleven-keg lagering cooler and a main cooler that can store up to fourteen kegs of homemade beer. He added hardwood floors and threw down some Oriental rugs, plus a sofa, table and bookcases. This is where he displays the biggest of his one-hundred-plus medals, including the AHA gold and four Best-in-Show medals from Lunar Rendezbrew competitions. He's joined the Bexar Brewers club there (as in Bexar— pronounced "Bear"—County, which includes San Antonio), but he still considers the Mashtronauts his home base.

Jurgensen and Heniff bring strong analytical and scientific skills to their brewing, but both insist that personality is just as much a part of the calculation. Heniff, turning philosophical, says that while brewing is a rewarding challenge and drinking good beer pleases the palate, building and maintaining relationships are the most satisfying pleasures of craft beer.

"Beer, throughout time, has always been a beverage that brings people together," he says. "That is far and away the best aspect of the hobby."

Jurgensen, a generation older, sees an even bigger picture, with a lot of overlap between home-brewers and other groups that "don't feel constrained by society's norms." Witness, he says, the number of long-distance bicyclists and convertible drivers who also brew. The same goes for the above-average number of space travelers and men with beards.

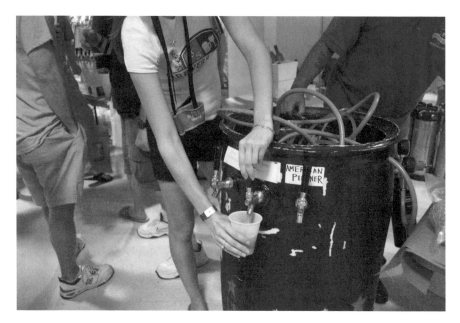

Lunar Rendezbrew is more than an awards ceremony. Local home-brewers show off their stuff. *Photo by Ronnie Crocker.*

"I think brewers as a group don't feel constrained to do things the normal way," he says. "Anyone who goes into space is not constrained to do things the normal way. It's not normal. Yet NASA felt it was worthwhile."

No surprise, then, that it was a home-brewer who figured out how to make craft beer sustainably viable in Houston on a commercial scale.

Chapter 8

Saint Arnold, Patron Saint of Houston Beer

Early-rising college students mingled with office workers taking a mid-morning lunch break in a line that formed early and grew steadily. Cars were still pulling into the parking lot when the doors to the store opened at ten o'clock. Then there was an orderly but determined march to the back, where the sales staff handed out rationed supplies until they were gone a mere twenty-one minutes later. This was September 10, 2009—two months before Black Friday shopping and seven months before the iPad made its impressive debut—so passersby en route to or from downtown's nearby skyscrapers might have wondered what the heck was going on. Why, there wasn't even a hurricane in the Gulf to send folks scrambling for plywood or bottled water.

"We're supporting Texas," explained Richard Fernandez, who waited in line with his friend Omar Akbar at the sprawling liquor warehouse known as Spec's. "Texas beer."

The occasion was the release of a strong, smoky Scotch ale from Houston's Saint Arnold Brewing Company, the eighth beer in its Divine Reserve series. At $14.99 a six-pack, Divine Reserve No. 8 was double the price of most craft-beer products and close to three times what mass-market brew would run. Yet the high cost deterred few Saint Arnold fans, and the most determined ones that day were rewarded with a flavorful, aromatic beer packed with seven different grains, hopped early and late with two varieties of German Hallertau hops and brewed to a potent 9.3 percent alcohol by volume. The beer not only was made in Texas, as Fernandez had noted, but it also was based on a contest-winning recipe from a local home-brewer, Phillip Kaufman of the Kuykendahl Gran Brewers.

Fans of Saint Arnold, accustomed to long lines for its limited-release Divine Reserve series beers, lined up early for the release of Pumpkinator in October 2011. In the foreground is Adrian Fuentez, who was first in line. *Photo by Ronnie Crocker.*

The popularity of these small Divine Reserve batches had grown steadily since the first one four years earlier, in the fall of 2005. But interest in DR8, as fans referred to the beer in desperate shorthand Twitter bursts during the ensuing social-media scavenger hunt, dwarfed all that had come before. And when DR9, an imperial stout spiced with pumpkin, was released with another 1,500-case run on December 1, it sold out at Spec's in just ten minutes.

The Houston beer scene had gone from abuzz to ablaze. Wine bars were hosting beer tastings, and new beer bars were opening with a laser focus on non-Bud, non-Miller and non-Coors products. Tony restaurants got in on the action by highlighting various craft breweries with elegant beer dinners. Even imports seemed passé. In December, a local attorney named Cathy Clark hosted the first of what became quarterly hard-to-find-beer tastings to raise money for a charity she'd founded to honor a friend who died young. The response was overwhelming, and tickets for subsequent Camp Beer events sold out in hours or sometimes just minutes.

In February 2010, two of the city's best beer bars were swamped for six straight nights when they teamed up for an alternating vertical tasting

Houston artist Shadi Farahani chalks some finishing touches on the newest Flying Saucer Draught Emporium, in the Houston suburb of Sugar Land. *Photo by Ronnie Crocker.*

of rare Russian imperial stouts from the cellared Southern California reserves of Stone Brewing Company. Jake Rainey, general manager of the Flying Saucer Draught Emporium, one of the "Stone'd for Six Days" partners, explained why it was good for business, even if the bars were encouraging customers to visit a competitor every other night: "We're going to expose people to some good beer. They're going to come back." He was quickly proven right. The atmosphere each Stone'd night was electric, and Rainey's co-host in the event, owner Ben Fullelove of the Petrol Station, found the bigger crowds did indeed stick around. A year later, his cozy pub tucked away in a quiet neighborhood bested 109 competitors to earn the designation America's "Most Bitter Bar" for selling more of Stone Brewing's hoppiest beers than any other place in the country.

These developments reflected a broader national trend, with consumer demand shifting toward American craft breweries—defined by the Brewers Association as smaller, independently owned breweries that use traditional ingredients almost exclusively, adding adjuncts only "to enhance rather than lighten flavor"—and a nasty recession that cut into the big beer companies' sales. Despite the economy and the stagnant to shrinking overall market for

Petrol Station owner Ben Fullelove (left) and Flying Saucer general manager Jake Rainey teamed up in 2009 for a wildly popular six-night tasting of rare Stone Brewing Company beers. *Photo by Nick de la Torre*/Houston Chronicle.

suds, the beer aisle at the grocery store grew longer and more crowded as the craft breweries exploded in number and popularity.

Houston, like Texas as a whole, was regarded as a latecomer to this revolution, but it was playing catch-up fast. Saint Arnold had outgrown the industrial park where it had opened in 1994 and was in the process of retrofitting a pre-Prohibition-era warehouse into a showcase brewing facility with a thirteen-thousand-square-foot addition to house the brew house and giant 240-barrel fermentation tanks, a spacious beer hall upstairs for public events and dramatic views of the downtown skyline. A second local craft brewery, Southern Star, an hour to the north in Conroe, was enjoying a robust second year in business, and rumors began to circulate that more were on their way. Stone CEO Greg Koch said of Texas, "I've been absolutely impressed with the shift I've seen in just the last two years."

Brock Wagner, the Saint Arnold founder, had survived the shakeout of the '90s that had claimed Houston's brewpubs and several of the state's production craft breweries by sticking to a carefully prepared

Kansas City–based Boulevard Brewing shows Houston some love at the Houston Distributing Company's first Brew Fest, an event designed to highlight craft beers handled by the company that once was strictly a Miller house. *Photo by Ronnie Crocker.*

business plan. When this boom came, his company was nearly perfectly positioned to take advantage of it. Wagner had staked everything he had on "handcrafted microbrewed" beer and then doubled down when the opportunity arose.

The Rice graduate and former investment banker is originally from Cincinnati and his family roots are in California, but he is at least a spiritual descendant of the early Houston brewers John Wagner and his half brother Peter Gabel. All shared a vision for a hometown brewery that would prosper by catering to the tastes of their generation. In the nineteenth century, Wagner and Gabel knew their city's German immigrants thirsted for the lagers of their homeland over the more prevalent ales, with their British heritage. In the 1990s, Brock Wagner and a business partner, Kevin Bartol, decided Houstonians again were thirsting for something new. This time, it would be an alternative to the increasingly light lagers that Swedish bikini teams and countless athletes-turned-pitchmen had convinced them they wanted.

They were playing more than a hunch, however, for Wagner and Bartol are men who always do their homework.

Brock Wagner had an enviable upbringing. His father was a successful corporate executive, first with Procter and Gamble and then Colgate, and the family was posted to Brussels during Wagner's formative preteen years. After the family returned home, Wagner was enrolled in an elite preparatory school, Cincinnati Country Day. Visits to see his grandparents in Northern California came with spectacular views of the Pacific Ocean from their lovingly landscaped homestead, which is now the Mendocino Coast Botanical Gardens. He enjoyed a warm relationship with his father, and the two became tennis partners who liked to split a single bottle of beer after matches.

Even without the National Merit Scholarship Wagner had earned, financing a top-notch college education wasn't going to be a problem. Neither would gaining admission. When the time to choose a school arrived, his options included Princeton and Rice. At eighteen, he was self-possessed enough to know he wanted to live on a coast, and he was struck by the egalitarian spirit he encountered on the campus in Houston. "If I go to Princeton after going to a prep school," he recalls thinking, "in a few years I won't like myself."

Saint Arnold founder Brock Wagner celebrated the opening of his new brewery with a ceremonial snip of the ribbon. *Photo by Brett Coomer/*Houston Chronicle.

A Heady History of Brewing in the Bayou City

Alcohol was another part of Wagner's family pedigree, and not just because of the trips to Burgundy wineries while the Wagners lived in Europe or the martinis and glasses of wine that were a frequent feature of family celebrations. A fourth-great-grandfather was a liquor merchant in Alsace, and a third-great-grandfather settled in New Orleans and San Francisco, working in the bar business in both places and, in 1861, founding a San Francisco saloon in a building in North Beach that now hosts a blues club. A cousin of his father owns a winery, and a 101-year-old grandfather tells stories of buying bootlegged whiskey for his classmates at Cal-Berkeley during Prohibition.

But the beer bug had yet to bite young Wagner when he arrived at Rice in 1983, and when it did, it was more of a nibble than a chomp. He came to Houston to study mechanical engineering, though he switched his major to economics. He hosted wine tastings but was intrigued by the imported beers at a Rice-area restaurant called Hungry's, where he had his first Pilsner Urquell from Czechoslovakia and his first beer from Scotland's Belhaven Brewery. "I started tasting all these beers from around the world," he says. "I thought, 'Why do we have to keep drinking light beers from kegs in the dorms?'" Before long, a friend was teaching him how to brew his own in those same campus dorms, a hobby that continued after graduation. Then, living on the eleventh floor of a high-rise apartment building, Wagner made beer in the kitchen, driving away his roommate on brew days. "I thought it was the most wonderful smell in the apartment and he thought it was the most awful smell," he explains.

"Stouts, porters and pale ales tended to be my standard brews," says Wagner. "I drank a bunch of Grölsch so I could get the swing-top bottles." Brewing got easier once he bought his own place, a four-plex, where he lived basically for free by taking one unit for himself and renting out the other three. Beer remained a hobby, however, and nothing more. He had a lucrative career as an investment banker, specializing in figuring out the value of oil-service companies.

"I thought my goal in life was to get rich," he says.

It took six and a half years in the real world to appreciate a lesson he'd been offered years before from his grandfather, who retired from the nursery business and then bought that property on the Mendocino coast. The old man spent his days in a khaki work shirt and pants, with a straw hat to shield him from the sun. He drove an old pickup truck and turned dirt to make his home into a gardener's paradise that people wanted to bring their kids to see. That was a life project he was truly passionate about and one that often caused him to turn philosophical. As a lifestyle, his was about as far removed from investment banking as one could imagine.

To hear Wagner tell it now, disillusionment with his early career came quickly. At one job, he felt pressured to tweak an analysis to inflate the value of a business deal to boost the size of the brokerage fee. In 1990, he was at the local office of Drexel Burnham Lambert when the firm disintegrated under the weight of the Michael Milken junk-bond scandal. Another Wall Street outfit, he says, brought him to New York for six months to learn the corporate culture and then tried to keep him from returning to Houston. Philosophical differences with his boss wore on him, and by the time he arrived in California for a family Thanksgiving get-together in 1992, Wagner was feeling miserable and a little philosophical himself.

"I started thinking about what my grandfather had said about loving what he did every day," he says.

He told his parents he thought he'd like to open his own brewery and followed up by studying financial reports for a couple of small breweries. On a Christmas trip back to California, he visited the Mendocino, Anderson Valley and North Coast breweries and talked to the owners. He partnered with Bartol, a Rice grad and Harvard MBA who had hired Wagner for his first job out of college. Bartol remembers Wagner as smart, quiet and even-keeled. The two had remained friends after Wagner moved on from that first job, getting together over beers like Anchor Liberty or Sierra Nevada Pale Ale. Bartol, too, was growing tired of the grind. "After a while," he says of investment banking, "everything is reduced to the dollar." Since high school, Wagner had wanted to someday start his own business. He and Bartol toyed with the idea of renovating lofts in downtown Houston or raising a herd of bison to capitalize on the healthy-eating trend.

Making beer was the only idea that stuck.

Wagner says he kept expecting pushback as he talked to people about a brewery project, but everyone seemed supportive of the idea. On January 8, 1993, he quit his job to pursue the quest full time. Headhunters would continue to call, but he had left investment banking for good.

At the time, there were only about one hundred shipping breweries in the United States. Wagner and Bartol went to Kansas City and sat down with Boulevard Brewing founder John McDonald. They made an expedition to the Pacific Northwest, which had become one of the country's hottest spots for craft beer. "I remember being taken aback at how friendly and helpful all the brewers were," Wagner says. The shoptalk focused on the technical aspects of making beer, and the Texans were struck that no one seemed much interested in marketing. Bartol recalls that when they pulled out copies of their business plan to see if they were using the right assumptions, the brewers seemed impressed, but it was obvious none had seen the need to do one himself. Bartol recalls the blank looks they got when they asked how to market their products. In Yakima, Washington, he says, pioneering microbrewer Bert Grant seemed incensed when asked why people bought his beer: "He looked at me like I was an idiot and he said, 'Because it's the best beer in the world.' I asked, 'How do they know? Does it say that on the package?' Then he looked at me like I really was an idiot."

"At that point," Wagner explains, "you didn't have to do anything to sell beer. There was so much demand and so little supply."

"Kevin and I knew Texas was not going to be that easy of a sell. But we had no idea how hard of a sell it would be."

Wagner and Bartol determined it would take $600,000 to build their brewery and they would need another $300,000 in working capital to get started. Despite being just twenty-nine and thirty-four, respectively, the paychecks that came with their former careers had left Wagner with about $125,000 in personal savings that he could put into the project and Bartol with about $350,000. Their backgrounds in finance helped again when they set out to raise the other half of the money. Wagner's father, Larry, the former P&G executive, helped them write a mission statement and guiding principles, and the partners set off to secure investors. This was in 1993, a year before the opening of Houston's first brewpub, and Shiner Bock was about as far from the mainstream as most local beer drinkers ventured. Wagner says they got turned down a lot before the fundraising suddenly took off and they eventually had to turn some people away.

"You get a couple of yeses and it's like everybody smells it," is how Wagner recalls it. A big break came while he was talking to a friend and former Drexel colleague about the $25,000 minimum investments the company was seeking. This friend's father had built an innovative Houston energy company that was on the verge of a breakout no one would forget, and the dad was destined to become as well known to his generation as Howard Hughes had been to an earlier one. The fiftyish chief executive walked in while his son and Wagner were going over the business plan, and he must've liked what he heard.

"Put me in for three units," said Ken Lay. Just like that, the founder of Enron Corporation, a mega-company whose name once graced the city's professional baseball stadium before its historic collapse and the ensuing criminal-fraud convictions of Lay and other executives, had effortlessly breathed a little life into the brewery project. Then he walked out of the room. His only caveat, recalls Wagner, was that the two young owners pay themselves less than $100,000 a year to begin with. That wasn't going to be a problem, as it turned out.

"We weren't paying ourselves diddly squat," Wagner says of the early years. "Most of our employees made diddly squat. It was a big deal when somebody's pay passed $20,000 back then."

Fundraising for Saint Arnold Brewing Company, named for a seventh-century bishop who famously advised his flock to drink beer because water wasn't safe, was completed by late summer. Bartol quit his banking job in September, and the following month he and Wagner ordered a thirty-barrel brew house. They got a lease on a bay in a light industrial park on an unremarkable stretch of road in the Loop 610 West–U.S. 290 area and started buildout on January 1, 1994. "We didn't invest a lot of money in the building because we knew we'd eventually move," Bartol says.

Their plan to begin selling beer in May hit a speed bump in April, during a city-mandated pressure test of the steam lines. The line to the brew kettle wasn't shut off, and the pressurized steam blew out the bottom of the $50,000 piece of equipment. It took a welder two weeks to tear down the brew kettle and put it back together. "It was a mess," Wagner recalls. Luckily, they say, the contractor's insurance paid for the repairs.

In the meantime, Wagner tried to stay focused on the beer the new company was going to sell. He was consulted by George Fix, a mathematics professor trained at Texas A&M, Rice and Harvard and a nationally renowned home-brewer who wrote numerous papers and books on the science of brewing. They refined recipes and experimented with several yeasts until they found one from a brewery in southern England that had the creamy, malt-forward characteristics Wagner was looking for. "That became our house strain," he says. Bartol recalls inviting people over for blind taste tests as the recipes were further tweaked. The first beer was Saint Arnold Amber, which remains a flagship, especially in the home Houston market. An early batch had to be dumped before the brewers figured out how to scale it up to a commercial level.

On June 9, 1994, the company filled its first kegs of Amber and trucked them out to four accounts: the Ginger Man, Star Pizza, Richmond Arms and JP Hops House. Houston was a two-newspaper town at this point, and coverage of that first day in business reflected the differences in the papers' approach. The *Chronicle* photo focused on the business end of the brewery, showing kegs being loaded for delivery, while the *Houston Post* opted for a shot of a smiling Bartol, who led the distribution and marketing end of the business, pouring a ceremonial first draft at the grand-opening party. It was a moment of triumph but also one of trepidation. That first Amber, says Wagner, was more like an India pale ale than it is today: "The home-brewers loved it."

But Wagner also recalls seeing a lot of half-empty glasses around the bar, abandoned by Houstonians who didn't know what to make of this new brew. Based on their preliminary interviews with bar owners, Wagner and Bartol had estimated they would need twenty accounts to hit their first-year target, but they soon found that they were selling only 25 percent of the beer they'd forecast. It seemed they were going to need to be in eighty accounts. They

Kevin Bartol, Wagner's partner in founding Saint Arnold in 1994, pours a pint of Amber on the brewery's first night in the marketplace. *Photo by Craig H. Hartley*/Houston Post.

got their second-hand bottling line running in September, and in that first partial year they sold 603 barrels' worth of beer, which was one-half of 1 percent above their modest target.

"It was really, really hard to sell people on our beer," Wagner says. "There just wasn't a craft beer market here."

The key to surviving during this period was to keep startup costs low and scrimp and haggle over everything else. "We watched every penny," says Wagner. "We were tight. We didn't waste any money. We ran a very tight ship."

As they had done with their building, forgoing anything as unnecessary as air conditioning or heating, the partners rejected expensive advertising campaigns in favor of a grass-roots marketing strategy. Bartol ran the roads to meet with accounts, he courted grocery store managers daily and he brought free beer to Kiwanis Club meetings. The first brewery tour was held the first Saturday the two were in business, Bartol says, and he made sure there was a clipboard on hand to collect email addresses to stay in touch with potential customers. Soon, they had a mailing list of five thousand people, enough for their blast emails to draw crowds to their pub crawls, which built brand loyalty with the drinkers and the bars that got to sell them beer. The effort was innovative for its time, given that the Internet wasn't the ubiquitous presence it is today. That list has since swelled to thirty-four thousand.

Despite the lack of air conditioning and its Spartan furnishings, the Saint Arnold brewery quickly became an attraction itself. Although state law prohibits manufacturers from selling beer on-site, it allows them to serve samples for free. In addition to hosting free Saturday tours, with open taps for visitors, Wagner and Bartol donated brewery parties to charity organizers to auction off in their fundraisers. These were cater-it-yourself affairs, and during the summer months the brewery could get quite warm, but they were always well attended. Free beer proved to be a big draw, even on the relatively few frigid days of winter, and Saint Arnold was eventually able to charge for the brewery rentals. Over time, during the nicest times of the year, it could be difficult to score a reservation.

Bartol estimates that during those first couple of years, Saint Arnold raised $300,000 to $500,000 for local charities—more than the company earned in profits—and built up long-term goodwill in the process. He recalls being out one day when someone shouted his name and thanked him for donating a keg to his running club. This occurred about five years after Bartol had left the company, but after talking with the guy, he remembered the event. "We gave them one keg. Exxon gave them probably $15,000," Bartol says. "He couldn't remember one guy at Exxon, but he remembered the guy who gave them that keg."

The company also put its first delivery truck, before there was enough business to require a distributor, on double duty. Bartol heard about an old Budweiser truck that was for sale in Virginia for $4,500, and he paid a guy $500 to drive it down. The truck didn't have air conditioning, but it ran well. A $5,000 paint job emblazoned the Saint Arnold logo on the sides and turned it into a bright red and metallic gold "rolling billboard."

"We had people regularly say, 'I saw one of your trucks!'" says Bartol. "We had one truck."

These organic marketing efforts were much more effective, he adds, than the $50,000 radio ad campaign they once paid for and quickly pulled.

Production grew rapidly, to 2,400 barrels in 1995 and to 4,200 in 1996. While Saint Arnold would outlive all of the Houston brewpubs and several Texas micros that were opening around the same time, success took longer than expected. In 1996, with Saint Arnold available in Houston and Austin and an expansion to Dallas next on the schedule, the brewers told a *Chronicle* business columnist they hoped to be selling more than 100,000 barrels within ten years. In reality, production hit 5,200 barrels that year and remained essentially flat for the next four years. The company would experience other growth spurts, but it wouldn't pass the 40,000-barrel mark until 2011.

Though they remain friends, the Saint Arnold founders could clash as business partners. Wagner approached Bartol as early as 1997 about buying him out. "The company wasn't big enough for the both of us," he says. Bartol says that by 1999, he was on the verge of burning out and did not want to be a negative influence. He left the company, though he retains a small stake and still talks with Wagner at least monthly. The company had built up some cash by this point, and Wagner borrowed half a million dollars to buy out the thirteen biggest investors. The old financial analyst estimated the value of Saint Arnold shares to be 70 cents apiece, but Wagner paid the original $1-a-share price.

"Everyone was very gracious about it," he says. "I remember Ken Lay told me, 'If my worst investment broke even, I'd be one hell of an investor.'"

The move boosted Wagner's stake in Saint Arnold to 70 percent, up from 15 percent; he and his father together owned close to 90 percent. It ushered in, Wagner says, "definitely a high-stress period" for him and for his seven employees. They brewed two double batches two days a week, filtered two days a week and bottled two days a week. "When we bottled, everybody was on the bottling line," he says. A young brewer at the time,

Dave Fougeron, recalls seventy-hour workweeks in the stifling summer heat. And Wagner notes there was more to do than just brew and bottle. The crew experimented with new beers and continued to spend time in the field, talking with store and bar owners. They manned the pub crawls, staffed the in-brewery parties and managed the increasingly popular Saturday tours. There was accounting and other office work.

"We didn't know what was going to happen here," says Wagner. "We just kept working."

Chapter 9

A Southern Star Rises to the North

This might sound familiar: Houston's brewing industry at the turn of the twenty-first century was dominated by two companies, one locally owned and the other headquartered in St. Louis. In further echo from one hundred years earlier, the beer business was again facing the headwinds of change. The clamorers this time were not prohibitionists or politicians, however, but beer drinkers themselves. They wanted more flavor and more variety. For anyone thinking of starting a brewery that catered to these new demands, there were far more fair-weather flags than warnings on the horizon.

One of the most encouraging developments, from the perspective of a survivor like Saint Arnold Brewing Company, was that the customer base was getting younger and more diverse. Once dominated by a thirty-and-older crowd, the so-called Saint Arnold Army was rapidly attracting customers in their twenties. Wagner theorizes this was a natural evolution in the U.S. craft movement, which had been building momentum for two decades and in which, locally, he had played an instrumental role. "Craft beer had been there at some background level," Wagner says, and it was now a mainstream phenomenon. "Basically, the market is moving toward us."

In 2001, the Houston brewery recorded its first significant increase in production after four years of relatively flat sales, a 23 percent surge, to 6,101 barrels. There was only a slight bump in 2002, due at least in part, Wagner suggests, to the sudden popularity of another amber ale, Fat Tire from Colorado's New Belgium Brewing Company. "Fat Tire," he says, "it was like they wrote a hit song. Everybody wanted a Fat Tire. I think they took some sales from us." But that brief lull was followed by a 17 percent jolt in 2003 that sparked a string of record-setting years. Between then and 2011, when Saint Arnold moved 40,416 barrels out the door, the annual growth rate reached as high as 31 percent; the rate dipped below 20 percent in only one year, 2009, and that was because of capacity constraints. The company had literally outgrown its brewery.

As the number of stainless-steel fermenting tanks multiplied across the brewery floor to keep up with production demands, Wagner recognized as early as 2005 that he was going to need a bigger facility sooner rather than later. In addition to its own lineup of year-round, seasonal and special-release brands, the company also was making beer for the BJ's chain of former brewpubs. Saint Arnold expanded into an adjacent space in the industrial park, but it was hardly adequate to keep pace with this growing demand. Twelve-hour shifts were not uncommon. "On brewing days, I was brewing," says Wagner. "On filtering days, I was filtering. On bottling days, I was bottling." He tried to start at 5:00 a.m. but found he wasn't a morning person. He worked instead from 6:00 a.m. until around 6:00 p.m. and then often headed out to promotional events in the evening.

"By the time I got there, it was, 'We need that beer yesterday,'" Bev Blackwood recalls of his two-year tenure at Saint Arnold. The beer writer and former *Malt Show* host had become an accomplished home-brewer in his own right and was hired in 2006 to supervise production at the brewery. He and Wagner had met as students at Rice two decades before, and Blackwood had promoted Saint Arnold products on his television program. Now, the two were in a business relationship, and the pressure to keep pace with sales was intense. "We were always running out of beer," he says. "The words we dreaded to hear were, 'We need that beer,' coming from Brock." The margin of error had shrunk to nearly zero. "As production started to reach capacity," Blackwood explains, "small mistakes had large consequences."

The work was physically demanding, as well. Former Saint Arnold brewer Dave Fougeron recalls jumping into a mash tun at the end of one shift to clean the filter screens and spray down the inside walls. But he hadn't let the tank cool adequately, and he got overheated. He knew he was in trouble when he stopped sweating and his head began to spin. "I felt woozy for days after that," he says, and in fact he still has to be careful when the mercury begins to climb. In another incident, Fougeron was working alone early one morning when a hose slipped out of his hand and he was scalded with 197-degree water. A maintenance man arrived and found him trying to crawl into a freezer. Fougeron was taken to the emergency room and found he'd suffered burns to 12 percent of his body. He missed two weeks of work.

A Heady History of Brewing in the Bayou City

Mother Nature could complicate matters with more than just brutal heat and cold. Wagner was on the brewery floor one night when lightning zapped a compressor on the roof, sending a surge of electricity through the chiller that blew out a copper pipe. The thunderclap and blowout were frightening, but no one was injured. In 2008, Hurricane Ike knocked out electricity to much of the city, in some neighborhoods for days or even weeks before utility crews could get to them. Saint Arnold lost power to its cold box, where some of its early Divine Reserve beers were stored. The crew kept the door closed, but the temperature climbed to seventy degrees before Wagner found a private electrician who could squeeze him onto the schedule.

"It was the best thousand dollars I ever spent," he said.

In 2006, Wagner got serious about finding a new facility. He was determined not to settle for a boring concrete box on the outskirts of town where the rent is cheaper, but that meant it would take a while before he found the perfect place. In February 2007, a friend told him about a three-story, red brick warehouse that offered easy access to Interstate 10 and fabulous views of downtown.

At the time it was built, in the 1910s, a person standing on the roof would've seen Buffalo Bayou and the chuffing smokestacks from the American and Magnolia Breweries in the near distance. More recently, the Houston public school district had been storing food there for its 200,000 students. The district was preparing to move that operation, and one of the Harris County commissioners intimated to Wagner's friend that no one wanted to buy the building and it was likely to be torn down. When Wagner went to see it for the first time, he could see why: "You'd tour this building, and it was scary."

But the brewer was smitten with the possibilities. That October, he outbid two other prospective buyers in a sealed-bid auction.

"This was one of those things where I had fallen in love with the building," Wagner says. The warehouse was close to the heart of the city, and its scarred and faded exterior offered instant character. On a more practical level, it was big enough to accommodate as much future expansion as Wagner decided he would ever attempt. As he explained at the time, "It's exactly what I've always wanted."

After running the numbers, Wagner decided he would need perhaps $500,000 in further investment to make the "newery" project work. In April 2008, he holed up in his office and wrote a prospectus. This time around, there was none of the reluctance to invest that he'd seen back in '94. Within two weeks, the company had raised $1.5 million; the total eventually reached $2.5 million. Wagner remained the majority owner, controlling 61 percent of

Saint Arnold Brewing Company completed its move into its new brewery in a retrofitted warehouse near downtown in 2010. From the roof you can see Buffalo Bayou and the site of the old American and Magnolia breweries. *Photo by Brett Coomer/*Houston Chronicle.

the business, but he now had 140 investors who had kicked in an average of $20,000 to $25,000 apiece. Many in this new crop had a personal connection with Saint Arnold that their predecessors lacked.

"We do have a lot more home-brewers," says Wagner. "A lot of the people who invest with us are our customers."

He paid $1.2 million for the warehouse and wound up putting in close to $8 million to transform it into a modern brewery. He and the school district closed on the deal in June 2008.

By then, Saint Arnold had its first local craft competitor.

One summer morning in 1997, Dave Fougeron got two phone calls, offering a stark choice to a young man who had finished college thinking he wanted to work in the environmental sciences until he discovered that "there were no positions for an ecological champion." If he zigged, Fougeron would wind up in Nevada studying to be a game warden. If he zagged, he'd be learning to brew beer professionally in Houston.

He picked brewing, he says, because, "I thought it would be really cool to make beer for a living." He became good at it, too, and went on years later to build a successful business as the owner of Southern Star Brewing Company. But he waxes philosophical about the decision he made when he was just twenty-four. "My life would've been a lot different if I had gone the other way," he says. "I think I would've been happy with that, too."

And he's probably right, for it is hard to imagine this little brother of four older sisters being anything other than pleased as punch in life. His tastes range from William Faulkner to Black Sabbath, and he has been known to break out an electric guitar to jam with the band during a party at the brewery. One "super-cool" job he held, during an interval between brewing gigs, was maintaining the disc-golf course in The Woodlands while working for the parks and recreation department there. Part of the attraction was getting off early enough in the day to play a round himself and talk about beer with friends over a cold one in the shade near the thirteenth hole.

Like a lot of craft-brew fans in their thirties and older, Fougeron remembers the beer that converted him. It was a Hacker-Pschorr Dunkle Weisse that he tried while a student at Texas A&M University in the early 1990s. "Pretty much right then and there I decided, 'Why does anyone drink that other stuff?'" He is now widely quoted as saying something very similar: "You'll never meet an ex–craft beer drinker."

It's more than a clever marketing line, for Fougeron didn't just jump on a bandwagon when he co-founded Southern Star in 2008. For most of a decade before that, he had played a behind-the-scenes role in creating a craft-beer culture in Houston. It was Brock Wagner who gave him that opportunity.

Dave Fougeron (left) celebrates Oktoberfest with Ash Rowell of Duff Beer Distribution. *Photo by Ronnie Crocker.*

Fougeron graduated from college in May 1997 and moved back home to Cypress. He was kicking around on a job-search website for A&M alumni when he saw an ad Wagner had placed to come make beer at Saint Arnold. He applied, even though as a home-brewer he'd yet to attempt an all-grain batch. That would come on Saint Arnold's thirty-barrel system. "It was terrifying for me," as he remembers it.

His Saint Arnold career began during one of the brewery's high-growth, all-hands-on-deck periods. Under head brewer Pete Nordloh, Saint Arnold was developing the Summer Pils and starting to bottle seasonal releases. Fougeron says Wagner "put me on the brew house pretty quick." He, too, was part of the routine that had him filtering beer on non-brew days and working the bottling line whenever it was time to bottle. (In fact, this experience wrestling with a balky '50s-vintage labeling machine would influence Fougeron's decision at Southern Star to can its beers: "That's part of the reason," he says. "I know what bottling entails.") He also remembers the quizzical looks he got when he told people he worked for a craft brewery and the un-self-conscious pride felt in doing so.

"I was very, very proud to be working there," he says. "I knew it was a privilege to be working there and be part of Texas's brewing history. Even back then."

But he was restless, too, and after two years he left Saint Arnold and returned to College Station. He distributed beer for a bit, worked in an environmental-testing lab, met the woman who would become his wife and then moved with her to The Woodlands, where he got the parks and recreation job. In 2001, Wagner called again, this time with an offer to be co-head brewer. "I started feeling that itch," recalls Fougeron.

The Houston brewery was entering another growth spurt, and twelve-hour days again were commonplace. Fougeron was working an early shift and getting off at 4:00 p.m. and still playing disc golf at Bear Branch Park. His golf partners included Brian Hutchins and Rob Martin, and their conversations on the thirteenth hole again turned to beer and, by late 2006 or early '07, to what it would take to open a brewpub. They couldn't get the numbers to a reasonable size—"We got up to about $5 million and said, 'That's not going to work'"—and the talk turned to starting a production brewery instead. Fougeron and Hutchins made test batches on the weekends. In March 2007, they filed papers to incorporate.

The only problem was, Fougeron was still working for Wagner at Saint Arnold.

"In the conflict of interest, he let me go," says Fougeron. "I don't blame him. I wish I'd handled it differently."

But Fougeron was committed to the new enterprise, and his focus turned to scrounging up equipment and developing a signature recipe. Out of nineteen test batches, he and Hutchins settled on one they'd made at the beginning, a hoppy beer that would become Pine Belt Pale Ale. They and their friends had floated that first keg, and says Fougeron, "We kind of knew we had a winner." They signed a lease for a large space in a pine-tree-framed industrial park on the northern outskirts of Conroe, with the first six months rent-free. Fougeron's dad alerted them to a mothballed brew house for sale on eBay. They bought fermenting tanks from Texas Hill Country brewer Real Ale. They brewed their first commercial batch in February 2008 and sold their first keg on March 24 to Molly's Pub in The Woodlands.

With that, the Houston area doubled its number of craft breweries.

The domestic beer market again was rapidly changing. Growing numbers of people were opting for craft beer and, whenever possible, locally made craft beer. In Houston, Saint Arnold and Southern Star would have this niche to themselves for a couple of years. Wagner, the first man in, was in the best position to capitalize on the sudden momentum. It had been a long time coming.

"It took us twelve years to get significant brand awareness, and we were the only game in town," he says.

Wagner had cash, he had a brewery under development that could potentially quadruple production within a few years and, as of February 1, 2009, he suddenly had a new distributor with a reach that was virtually unmatched in the entire nation. In acquiring the assets of Glazer's, Houston-based Silver Eagle Distributors found itself with a new portfolio of unfamiliar craft beers, many of them with funny names and unorthodox sales pitches. Soon, eighteen-wheelers emblazoned with the familiar Anheuser-Busch logos were pulling away from the warehouse with the likes of Saint Arnold and Sierra Nevada on board. Saint Arnold, a company that had relied on grass-roots, word-of-mouth and, more recently, social media marketing, soon would be featured on a billboard overlooking the busy Interstate 45.

"I see the relationship between the brewer and the distributor and the retailer in terms of marketing," says John Nau, who came to Houston in

1987 and has overseen the growth of Silver Eagle into not only Anheuser-Busch's single largest distributor but also the second-largest of any kind in the nation.

Nau acknowledges that incorporating craft brands required "a significant learning curve" that lasted at least eighteen months. The company that was used to handling some twenty-three million cases a year of Bud Light suddenly was doing business with twenty or so suppliers that wouldn't sell five thousand cases. And these new brews had little in common with the light American lagers that dominated the Anheuser-Busch line. "We had to learn the difference between a Belgian wheat and ales and everything in between," says Nau.

As work began on his new brewery, Wagner found himself too pinched for space to take full advantage of this new distribution network. In 2009, the company's last year in its industrial-park bay, Saint Arnold grew by just 13 percent, selling 25,710 barrels of beer, but it wasn't for lack of demand. Wagner was eager to get into the "newery," as he took to calling it. But the move was slowed by everything from vandals, who broke into the construction zone and did thousands of dollars' in damage to steal a few hundred dollars' worth of copper piping, to a truck driver who banged up a brand-new brew kettle from Germany. The driver who picked it up at the Port of Houston took the wrong route out, Wagner says, and the oversized cargo struck an overpass.

At the brewery site, construction workers built a thirteen-thousand-square-foot addition to house the brewing equipment and towering new

John Nau III owns Silver Eagle Distributors, the largest Anheuser-Busch InBev distributor in the country. Silver Eagle now has a growing portfolio of craft beers as well. *Photo by Ronnie Crocker.*

fermentation tanks that were being craned into place, while other crews cleaned up the interior of the old food-storage warehouse and brought it up to code for public occupancy. They converted the second floor into an open beer hall, and longtime employee James Cunningham painted a beautiful Saint Arnold mural that would greet visitors at the hospitality bar. In addition to the extra space, the coming crowds would enjoy two things they'd done without in the old digs: air conditioning and ample bathrooms.

On October 28, some two hundred local dignitaries, politicians, longtime accounts and other guests were invited in to inspect the progress and christen the hospitality hall. Wagner, most often seen around the brewery in shorts and T-shirts, dressed up for the occasion in khaki trousers, a blue long-sleeve shirt and a pair of cowboy boots to meet and greet and snip the ceremonial ribbon.

The general public was supposed to get its first look the following Saturday, but this time it was city inspectors who delayed things by ordering a series of structural modifications before they'd issue a temporary occupancy permit. Wagner had already suspended tours at the old brewery, however, and the city's unexpected action pushed back "newery" tours to the end of December. The company would go two months without what Wagner calls "our single most important marketing tool."

Production switched to the new brewery on March 1, 2010. Three new 240-barrel fermenters meant capacity was no longer the immediate issue, but meeting demand still proved challenging. Summer Pils sold out on store shelves before it could be replaced as the brewers struggled to master the new system and work out kinks. Technicians were called in from Germany to help calibrate the equipment, and yet, despite these hiccups during the start-up, sales jumped another 22 percent as Saint Arnold surpassed thirty thousand barrels for the first time. By the end of the year, Saint Arnold was shipping its first beers out of state, to New Orleans, Baton Rouge and other cities in neighboring Louisiana. Wagner said at the time he had no intentions of expanding beyond there, and he gave a simple reason for this one foray beyond the eastern border: "Louisiana is closer to us than most of Texas."

Around that time, a national beer magazine put Saint Arnold on its list of "breweries to watch" in 2011. Sure enough, the new year was full of new beginnings.

As demand continued to surge, Wagner sold six of the 60-barrel fermenters that had come from the old brewery and replaced them with eight more of the 240-barrel tanks. He also dropped his slowest-selling beer, Texas Wheat, in favor of a new one called Weedwacker, which had proven popular in a limited-release run the previous year. It was the first release in a four-part series he dubbed "Movable Yeast," in which the brewers took a beer from the regular lineup and brewed it with a different strain of yeast to demonstrate how this unheralded ingredient—far less understood by the public than hops or malt—could affect taste. Weedwacker, a draft-only variant of the lighter-bodied and best-selling Fancy Lawnmower Kölsch, was pitched with a Bavarian hefeweizen yeast. This was, ultimately, the most popular beer in the series. The bottles began to roll out in May with labels that looked like Lawnmower's, except the manicured lawns of the original were now pocked with weeds.

In the fall, Saint Arnold launched a hybrid "black Kölsch" that also used Lawnmower as its base but used darker malts to give it at least a heavier appearance. Though Wagner said the beer wasn't aimed specifically at the city's growing Hispanic market, the packaging boasted a bold Day of the Dead–style artwork by local artist Carlos Hernandez and was the first not to feature the iconic robed Saint Arnold imagery. In its place, the "Santo" was presented as a skull wearing a golden crown. (Wagner was a fan of Hernandez's "Day of the Dead Rock Stars" series and has a wall-size original of a skeletal John Lennon hanging in his office.)

The Santo release was delayed by more than six weeks when the initial batch didn't meet specifications and had to be dumped. Expecting strong sales, Wagner had brewed more than he normally would for an initial launch, which meant eleven thousand gallons literally went down the drain.

"That probably goes down as a disappointment," he says, with a wry grin.

If so, it may have been the year's only one. Sales jumped 29 percent in 2011, with all Saint Arnold brands gaining in all of the company's distribution areas. Sales shot up 47 percent in Houston alone during November. Emblematic of this enthusiasm was the scene outside Spec's on the morning of October 13. The imperial pumpkin stout that had debuted in 2009 as Divine Reserve No. 9 was back, this time in twenty-two-ounce bomber bottles and renamed Pumpkinator. Though it would now be available in larger quantities as a recurring seasonal beer, some twenty people had already lined up when the doors opened at 10:00 a.m. One of them, twenty-four-year-old Adrian Fuentez, a veteran of three Divine Reserve releases, had been there since 7:00 a.m. and was not taking any chances of missing out. He was first in line.

The brewery tours—Bartol remembers being thrilled that twenty people came out for the first one—were now averaging close to one thousand people every Saturday. Monday-through-Friday tours, which had been added for the "newery," were up 90 percent in 2011, averaging around one hundred visitors daily. The crowds seemed further vindication of Wagner's observation that craft beer had arrived in the mainstream.

"You see everyone here," he says. "Students. You see teachers, lawyers. You see people from the Medical Center here. Truckers. It's just a huge melting pot.

"What I love about Houston is it's a giant melting pot and everybody gets along better than in any city I've ever seen. And Saint Arnold is a microcosm of that."

Wagner feels being part of that community is so important that he wrote it into his company's mission statement. Not only is the goal to brew and sell great beer, he says, but to "create an institution that Houston is proud of." It's a long-term strategy that could help the brewery achieve the enduring success that eluded his predecessors.

"I definitely want to create an institution that lives on," he says. "I hope Saint Arnold is around one hundred years from now."

Fougeron, meanwhile, was proving he could draw a crowd to Conroe. There amid the pine trees, in a small town with a laid-back East Texas vibe, just a few miles too far from Houston to be considered either suburb or even exurb, the brewer had surrounded himself with friends and what seemed like room to grow. Disc-golf buddies were among the investors, and some were on the payroll. Commemorative flying discs on the wall above the hospitality bar pay tribute to their role in Southern Star's history. Running the website is a guy Fougeron has known since he was about eleven years old. Physically, the busy brewery resembles the original Saint Arnold plant in its austere functionality; the picnic tables and mounted ram's head by the souvenir T-shirts give it the same feel of a "man cave," a place where friends like to hang out. On Saturdays, crowds of up to 350 people show up for beer, brats and barbecue. The tours are still free, but the ticketed Oktoberfest and anniversary parties sell out well in advance.

The brewery's strong three-beer lineup is anchored by the wildly popular Bombshell Blonde, which is often cited along with Saint Arnold's Lawnmower and Real Ale's Firemans #4 as among Texas's best "gateway" beers to the craft side of the market. This was the second offering from Southern Star,

Responsible for 70 to 80 percent of sales, Bombshell Blonde is Southern Star's moneymaker. *Photo by Billy Smith II/*Houston Chronicle.

sandwiched between the Pine Belt Pale Ale and Buried Hatchet stout, and it became the company's biggest seller by a large margin. It composes about 70 percent of the brewery's sales, and Fougeron says during summer that share can jump closer to 80 percent.

Bombshell Blonde may be Southern Star's moneymaker now, but it owes its existence to Tommy Bahama. The upscale retailer of casual wear has a restaurant in The Woodlands, just a few miles south of the brewery, and, in 2008, was looking for someone to make the blonde ale it served on tap. Fougeron tried the recipe the chain's previous supplier had been using and decided he could do better. The beer was well received by both the restaurant's management and customers alike. "Word got out that we were making a blonde ale," Fougeron recalls of the reception, "and everybody wanted to get the blonde ale." In October 2008, Bombshell hit the market under the Southern Star name in striking blue twelve-ounce cans that feature a blonde cowgirl riding a missile a la Slim Pickens in *Dr. Strangelove.*

Southern Star brewed for Tommy Bahama for nearly two years, and Fougeron says those four kegs a week helped keep his business afloat. He and Hutchins worked without pay for the first year and did practically everything around the brewery themselves. "I learned a lot about construction," he says.

"For the first year and a half, every time the rent was due we flirted with bankruptcy."

But by 2011, Fougeron, like Wagner, was in expansion mode. "Demand far exceeded supply," he says. Empty space on the brewery floor steadily gave way to new fermentation tanks, including three of those sixty-barrels that Saint Arnold was unloading and a new high-speed canning line that boosted annual capacity to around ten thousand barrels. The new line also allowed Southern Star to begin packaging its seasonal offerings. Because the brewery couldn't produce any of these yearly releases in enough quantity to justify the cost of buying cans in bulk and

After being hired as head brewer at Southern Star Brewing Company, Jeff Hamm made an immediate impact with two well-received seasonal brews, Walloon and Le Mort Vivant. *Photo by Ronnie Crocker.*

storing the unused ones until the season returned, the brewery devised a single can for use with all of them. They're green, with a "Season-Ale" logo, and they come with a clear adhesive strip inscribed with the name of the beer that is attached to each can by hand. It's a time-consuming task, but Fougeron ended the year with plans to increase production of the Season-Ales in 2012.

In the meantime, Hutchins left the day-to-day operations, and Fougeron hired two young brewers, including a Texas A&M graduate named Jeff Hamm as head brewer. Hamm, who graduated with a degree in biology, made an immediate impact with Southern Star's first two seasonals, a refreshing Belgian ale summer release called Walloon and a late-fall French Bière de Garde. In December, Le Mort Vivant was the first beer sold in a Season-Ale can. Total production for the year reached 5,200 barrels, up around 40 percent.

Fougeron also began scouting locations for a new brewery site once his current lease expires in the spring of 2013. He and Hutchins used to say

Beer dinners have grown in popularity. In 2010, Southern Star Brewing was the featured beer. Traci Davies (left) was one of the attendees. *Photo by Johnny Hanson/*Houston Chronicle.

they came to Conroe for the good water and the cheap rent, but Conroe has been good to Southern Star, and Fougeron says he intends to remain there. He's been careful with his money, too, growing at a manageable pace and avoiding excessive debt. He lived through the last shakeout, while at Saint Arnold, and wants to make sure he's not overextended when the next one comes. He feels good about 2012, when he expects production to grow to nine thousand or so barrels, but he wonders what 2013 will be like. Craft beer has been red hot, but a lot of new breweries have opened or been announced. It sounds a little too familiar.

"Then again, it's a different world," Fougeron says. "Nobody sees craft beer as a fad now."

Nor has the brewer betrayed any signs of waning enthusiasm. Fougeron remains as animated as ever.

"I still feel that way," he says, when asked about the unfiltered pride he knew while manning the brew house at Saint Arnold. "Something special is going on. This could be the golden age of Texas craft brewing."

Chapter 10

"Nobody Sees Craft Beer as a Fad Now"

The number of local craft breweries doubled again in 2011. First to market was a small family-run operation in one of the city's western suburbs, with an energetic but inexperienced young brewer at the helm. Early on, he made some expensive rookie mistakes, but he worked through them and managed to beat his own first-year sales forecast. Brian Royo's work ethic, his family story and the sheer enthusiasm he and his wife brought to their project made the brewery an easy one to root for. By the time the calendar rolled over again, No Label Brewing Company had a growing lineup of beers and plans in place for tripling production in its second year. It also had established itself as a Saturday afternoon destination in a former farm town now better known for its comfortable subdivisions, successful high school football teams and massive outlet mall along the interstate.

Several months later, another brewery roared to life with much different expectations. Experience wasn't an issue, as the founders were successful veterans of nearly three decades in the beer-distribution and importation business. They already owned a building that could readily be converted to a brewery, they had a muscular, tightknit organization in place and they possessed the means and clout to lure a top American brewer away from that craft-beer mecca known as Colorado. Long before Karbach Brewing Company put its first batch to boil, in-the-know beer fans were buzzing over the impending arrival of former Flying Dog CEO Eric Warner, a traditionally trained brewmaster who had literally written the book on wheat beers. The city responded enthusiastically when Karbach's beers went on tap, and the company exceeded its own comparatively aggressive projections for production.

No Label Brewing Company became the third craft brewery in the Houston area when it sold its first commercial pint in December 2010. Just over a year later, there were five, with another expected to open in just a few months. *Photo by Billy Smith II/*Houston Chronicle.

Nor was the expansion finished. Buffalo Bayou Brewing Company, founded by Rassul Zarinfar, another Rice grad with an MBA from Harvard, sold its first beer on January 27, 2012. At the same time, a group of friends who'd already built a successful business with a gourmet food truck had their state license in hand and were nearing completion of yet another microbrewery in Houston. This one was to be called 8th Wonder Brewing, in homage to the Astrodome. Other young entrepreneurs were openly discussing projects that ran the spectrum from a tiny neighborhood brewery where people could hang out during daily tours to a brewpub in a funky, turreted house overlooking the freeway that runs from downtown on the way to Bush Intercontinental Airport. Meanwhile, down in Galveston, two other young guns opened a bar called Brews Brothers in the downtown tourist area with plans to begin making beer on-site once they raised enough money to bring in equipment.

The Houston area was again awash in beer. The excitement generated by the newcomers benefited the existing crafts, whose final 2011 production reports were all full of good news. Restaurants, even those of the "white tablecloth" variety, increasingly came to regard craft beer as good for business, as Audrey Kiefer learned as Texas sales manager for California's North Coast Brewing Company. "All the intelligent business owners," she says, "are seeing you get a higher markup and a higher margin."

As more breweries were announced and store shelves swelled with new beers from elsewhere in Texas and from out of state, a group of Houstonians organized to try to accelerate growth in the industry even further. The founders of Open the Taps set out to raise funds to hire lobbyists who could

Audrey Kiefer has watched the Houston beer scene grow, first as a waitress at the Flying Saucer and now as Texas state sales manager for North Coast Brewing Company of California. *Photo by Ronnie Crocker.*

fight for changes in the state's alcohol laws. They were galvanized by the stalled legislative effort to allow take-home beer after brewery tours, which they felt demonstrated the undue influence of big beer on the political process, but their agenda included a broader array of consumer-focused issues. Meanwhile, a group of plaintiffs led by Austin newcomer Jester King Craft Brewery convinced a federal judge to throw out a pair of long-standing regulations that limited competition and hamstrung small brewers' marketing efforts.

In the meantime, other craft breweries were opening across the state, particularly in and around Austin, and those already open were enjoying the similarly robust growth seen in the Houston area. Real Ale Brewing joined Saint Arnold among the nation's fifty largest crafts, and Austin Beerworks scored a silver medal in its Great American Beer Festival debut. InBev's takeover of Anheuser-Busch moved Gambrinus's Spoetzl Brewery in Shiner up a notch among the biggest American-owned brewing companies. Shiner, too, increased the number of offerings, including, in early 2012, its first pale ale.

The activity seemed to underscore Dave Fougeron's observation. Maybe, as he said, this really was the golden age of Texas brewing.

The Royos were running a little behind schedule. It was still rush hour at 6:00 p.m. when they arrived downtown in Jennifer's little Toyota Corolla packed with half a dozen ⅙-barrel kegs, jockey boxes, CO_2 canister, tap handles and glass mugs inscribed with the No Label logo. They found a parking spot on the street, but maneuvering through the crush of homeward-bound office workers was difficult. Yet the young couple were their usual ebullient selves by the time the dinner showcasing the beers they'd brought in from Katy got underway at Ziggy's Bar and Grill. They were still running at full throttle when the waitstaff dished up dessert in those No Label mugs.

Brian Royo gave a little background on the beers to the twenty or so diners who'd paid fifty dollars each for the paired, five-course meal. The first one brewed, Royo said, was a traditional hefeweizen, which had been a favorite style of his wife before her inner hophead revealed itself. They named it El Hefe, a play on a Spanish term that is widely understood in both languages. "El jefe, the boss, that's her," said Brian. Then there was the Ridgeback amber ale, named in honor of the couple's dog, Hailey. And during a break, Jennifer Royo explained that they expected to soon have label approval for a new winter seasonal, a milk stout they were calling the Elda M. The style was a favorite of her mother-in-law, Brian's mom, and the Elda M was the name of a much-loved deep-sea fishing boat that her dad owned while she was growing up in Panama. It was a source of many fond memories.

Business is personal at No Label, the third craft brewery to open in the Houston area. Brian Royo brews, with one assistant and two part-timers, and Jennifer handles publicity and social media, though she's yet to quit her full-time marketing job. They co-own the brewery with Brian's parents, Gilberto and Melanie Royo, and they decided to call the business No Label because they feel their family, with its roots in Panama, Texas and Philadelphia, isn't

Brian and Jennifer Royo, owners of No Label Brewing Company in Katy, made their first appearance at the Great American Beer Festival in 2011. *Photo by Ronnie Crocker.*

easily labeled. They set up shop in Katy, the town west of Houston where the elder Royos settled while Brian was in high school, a town that is expected to continue to benefit economically from Houstonians' westward march.

Their first year in business, Brian and Jennifer seemed to be everywhere—from a hometown home-brew competition to the GABF in Denver to numerous bars, tastings and beer dinners like the one at Ziggy's—and always together, always smiling, the wholesome public face of the company.

Brian Royo dabbled in home-brewing while in college, a ten-year sojourn that led him ultimately to the University of Houston, where he met Jennifer, a fellow student, in 2004. After graduation, he got a job as a construction supervisor, and he and Jennifer eventually settled in Katy. Home life was great, but work was wearing him down. Brian enjoyed building things, but he hated the combative world of contractors and suppliers. "Every day was another fight with someone else," he says. Throw in the hour-plus commute in his Dodge pickup to Baytown on the opposite side of Houston, a trip that often included a cell-phone argument with someone about work, and it didn't take long for Royo to decide that making beer would be a more pleasant alternative.

After committing to the project, he and Jennifer, in tribute to Katy's agricultural heritage, leased an old, unused rice dryer along the railroad tracks. They moved in a small-batch brewing system and were inviting the public out for samples as early as August 2010, four months before they sold their first beer.

"There's no real attraction to come to Katy except to live," says Brian. "I wanted to bring some kind of attraction here."

His plan worked almost too well. The outdoor festivities quickly became so popular that they cut into Brian's time for brewing, and the Royos decided to suspend them until they got their full commercial system in place and running the following May. That, too, came with a steep and costly learning curve. For example, the first three or four batches didn't turn out right, and it wasn't until Brian was able to "reverse engineer" the process that he figured out the brew kettle hadn't been properly calibrated. Each dumped batch cost $1,000 to $1,500 in ingredients alone.

Royo also had to figure out how to estimate output for the year, again by trial and error. No Label wound up selling 800 barrels in 2011, twice as much as he'd planned for and close to the 900 barrels he'd predicted for 2012. If he was going to get it wrong, at least he'd erred on the conservative side. Given the way the first year turned out, though, he revised his second-year forecast upward to 2,500 to 3,000 barrels. He plans to build a core group of four or five accessible year-round beers with broad appeal—that means leaning to the lighter, refreshing side—and to mix things up with seasonals and one-offs that are bolder, hoppier, even "extreme."

No Label caught a break early on when John Anderson, a local home-brewer eager to make a career in beer, brought over some of his work and volunteered countless hours helping Brian brew. He worked an early shift at a Target store nearby and would swing by after he got off at 3:00 p.m., often brewing until 10:00 or 11:00 p.m. He did that for a year before the Royos were able to put him on salary.

The couple also benefited from their affiliation with their alma mater. Brian had been active on campus while a student, and he still cooks with a UH barbecue team during the annual cook-off that kicks off the Houston Livestock Show and Rodeo. During the brewery's gestation period, the Royos took samples from early test batches to tailgate parties during the Cougars' home football games; all they asked from people in exchange was feedback. Brian says his UH connections helped the couple get "preferred vendor" status there and have helped spread the word through word of mouth. "I don't know if we could've gotten where we are without those connections," he says.

Or without a lot of hard work. In addition to making beer and making the rounds to talk it up, the Royos resumed their "dog and kid friendly" Saturday tours and soon were swamped with crowds that often topped 500 and caused long lines for beer. The popularity of the tours again became a strain on the tiny company, which was going through as many as ten to twelve kegs each weekend and losing money in the process. In November, the Royos began charging $5, which brought the crowds down to a more manageable average of 270 to 280 each week. Jennifer sells around $1,500 worth of merchandise each tour, putting the money back into No Label's marketing account.

The Royos took on investors during 2011, but the family still owns 75 percent of the business, Brian says. He began negotiations for a twelve-thousand-square-foot warehouse, which could delay plans to begin bottling beers come summer. He, too, is optimistic about 2012, but he admits to a nagging concern about a possible beer glut in the two years after that. No Label won't always be the new brew that everybody is curious about, and the fight for tap space and shelf space could get as sharp-elbowed as the construction industry he left behind.

"I'm afraid there may be too many coming on too quickly," he says.

When Eric Warner went to Germany to study brewing in the late 1980s, no one was interested in hearing about the beer scene back home in the United States. "I remember more people talking about American politics," he says. "That was what I got grilled about mostly."

That probably would've been the case in most of America then, too, though maybe not in Colorado, where he grew up, or in Portland, Oregon, where he majored in German at Lewis and Clark College. For the most part, Americans had yet to embrace beers that weren't lightened with adjuncts and heavily promoted during ballgames. Even his parents, once their son told them he wanted to make beer professionally, tried to steer him toward a career with Coors or Anheuser-Busch.

But Warner had other inspirations. He drank his first Moosehead in high school and tried Beck's Dark by senior year. Moving to the West Coast for

Former Flying Dog CEO Eric Warner came to Houston as brewmaster of the startup Karbach Brewing Company. His intention was to make great beers, one after the other. *Photo by Johnny Hanson/*Houston Chronicle.

college, he says, "That opens up a whole new world of beers." Then came the day the owner of the pizza joint he worked at after graduation took the staff to visit some local craft breweries, including Widmer.

"I thought that tour was amazing and thought I'd like to learn more about this," he says.

For Warner, "learning more about this" meant cannon-balling into the deep end. He got with the study-abroad coordinator at Lewis and Clark who'd helped him with an earlier trip to Germany to find out if he could go back to study beer. He discovered the Technical University of Munich at Weihenstephan, a free-tuition university where he could do just that in a renowned brewing program. He moved to Bavaria and slogged his way from brewery to brewery until he found one that would hire him for the apprenticeship he needed before he could enroll. "I went knocking on doors in Bavaria," he recalls, "and got some of the strangest looks." And he became expert enough in the craft that he could write an acclaimed book on wheat beers that has remained in circulation for twenty years.

Within a decade of completing his studies at the Weihenstephan, Warner was part of the reason people could no longer dismiss American beer.

Warner was born in Denver in 1964. His mother, with whom he lived after his folks divorced, was a social worker. His father ran a mortuary, where Warner part-timed in high school and during the summers while home from college. Though he worked the reception desk mostly, he spent enough time in the prep room to see cadavers that had been reduced to "nothing but a spine and a pool of blood."

There would be no following in the family trade. After his beer epiphany in Portland and his formal beer education in Germany, he embarked on a passionate career that has now spanned a quarter of a century.

He did some work for the Institute for Brewing Studies and helped put on the Great American Beer Festival. He helped start a brewpub in Yellowknife, Northwest Territories, Canada, where he had to drill into a frozen river to pump out water. In 1992, he wrote the well-received *German Wheat Beer*, the seventh book in the Classic Beer Style series. He and three other men raised enough money to found Tabernash Brewing Company in 1993, and they were soon being toasted by the craft-beer elite. Tabernash Weiss took gold at the 1994 GABF in the German wheat ale category and two years later was named "domestic beer of the year" by *Malt Advocate* magazine. But keeping men in their twenties and early thirties—and still full of testosterone, as Warner notes—together proved problematic, and the group broke apart. Tabernash merged with Left Hand Brewing Company, which has gone on to achieve a somewhat exalted status of its own.

In 1999, Warner joined Flying Dog Brewing Company, which was selling around ten thousand barrels a year with spotty distribution. He rose from brewmaster to CEO before he left in 2008, when Flying Dog moved production to Maryland. During his tenure, the brewery released such beers as Snake Dog IPA, Double Dog double pale ale, Gonzo Imperial Porter and Dogtoberfest Märzen. It had grown into a respected national brand, pumping out fifty thousand barrels annually. Around the time he was leaving, he heard from one of his distributors that two guys down in Texas were looking to open their own brewery and might want to talk to him.

"Sure enough," says Warner, "I got a call from Ken Goodman out of the blue, summer of 2008."

Twenty-five years earlier, Goodman and Chuck Robertson had started the CR Goodman distributorship in Texas. They had a warehouse on Karbach Street in a light-industrial area of Houston, not far from where Saint Arnold would set up shop in 1994. Robertson's son, Blake, recalls how hard the men worked, delivering beer in their personal trucks in a pinch. The partners built a profitable business that included another distributorship in Colorado and

Belekus Marketing, which imported beers from such European breweries as Belhaven, Malheur and Bitburger. It covered most of the United States from its headquarters in College Station.

Goodman and Robertson sold their Texas distributorship, with its line of craft beers, to Ben E. Keith in 2008, freeing themselves under Texas law to pursue a production brewery. But this was at the beginning of a nasty recession—Warner recalls meeting David Greenwood, a former CR Goodman general manager who would run the sales and marketing side of Karbach, in September, as Lehman Brothers was melting down—and the project stalled for two years. But Warner, thinking he would be involved as a consultant, made a trip to Houston and was struck that the nation's fourth-largest city had a single craft brewery inside the city limits. With the nearest competitor nearly an hour away, he felt the market was ripe for another brewery.

Warner had a few other projects going during this time—he bought and sold a bar and helped with a whiskey distillery—but his attention shifted to Texas in 2010, when the Belekus crew "pulled the trigger" on hiring an architect to draw up designs for converting the Karbach Street warehouse into a brewery and making a down payment on equipment. By April 2011, the forty-seven-year-old brewmaster was mixing test batches in Houston and putting his home in the suburbs of Denver up for sale. His wife and two sons would join him shortly, in the midst of Texas's worst drought on record. Good thing, he says, his wife was over the Colorado cold.

As Hughes Tool had done at the close of Prohibition, Karbach Brewing Company brought money and high-profile talent to the worthy task of making beer. Warner, like Frantz Brogniez, was a formally trained master brewer with a track record of success. In Goodman and Robertson, he had deep-pocketed partners who could sink more than $1 million into building a first-rate brewery and give him a free hand in designing the place. They were savvy beer men who understood the distribution side of the business and had a strong team already in place. With an assistant named Chris Fall helping him in the fully automated brew house, Warner was overseeing the brewing end of a project that had capacity on day one to make four thousand barrels a year and push the Houston beer scene to a new level.

"We certainly had high expectations for ourselves," says Warner.

As they made the rounds on launch night, September 1, he, along with Goodman, Robertson and the rest of the Karbach crew, toasted to their success and bought beers for their new customers. An enthusiastic crowd at the Petrol Station quickly dispatched the first keg of Hopadillo IPA. Customers raved about Warner's latest creation, the hybrid Weisse Versa,

Karbach co-owner Chuck Robertson (foreground) as brewmaster Eric Warner works on a test batch during the Houston craft brewery's setup phase. *Photo by Brett Coomer/*Houston Chronicle.

pitched with a German hefeweizen yeast but brewed with coriander and citrus peel in the Belgian wit style. The "aggressively hopped" Sympathy for the Lager would make its impressive debut a few weeks later, just as the brewery was beginning to wow the market with potent pours like Rodeo Clown imperial IPA and Hellfighter imperial porter. By early in 2012, Karbach beers were on tap in 140 establishments, and the company was on schedule to produce 3,100 barrels in its first twelve months in business. The pace would no doubt pick up once the canning line went live the following March and nine new fermentation tanks arrived in June.

The dynamic changed with Karbach's arrival, as anyone following the local beer scene could tell. Houston had matured as a beer town. There's no telling what Peter Gabel, Frantz Brogniez and Charles Lieberman would have thought of Houston's newest wildcatters of ale. The distinguished gentlemen might not approve of the new generation's preference for short pants and short-sleeve work shirts over coats and ties. They might even think the new beers taste funny—too hoppy, too strong.

But they no doubt would be pleased to know that Wagner and Warner, Fougeron and Royo were carrying on their legacy in the Bayou City.

A Brief Epilogue

Not that anyone asked why during the reporting phase of this project, but there are several good reasons to write a book about the history of brewing in Houston. One is practical. Craft beer is a red-hot topic right now, and the editors at The History Press think a book like this will be popular.

A more high-minded rationale might be that people need to know their history in order to understand their present. Certainly, echoes become evident in the ebbs and tides of the beer industry.

But the best reason might be just this: it's one heckuva yarn, not widely known, rich and full of great characters. A century and a half before Brock Wagner decided he'd be better at making beer than raising bison, a teenager from Germany named Peter Gabel was embarking on one of those outsized immigrant adventures that have made this country a better place. Another larger-than-life character, Frantz Brogniez, moved to Houston from another state, bringing his family and a stellar national reputation in brewing— exactly ninety-nine years before Eric Warner did the same thing. And isn't it interesting to know that Howard Hughes and Ken Lay each played a role in fostering the local beer scene?

Can these contemporary figures tell us exactly what will happen next in Houston beer? Of course not. "The crystal ball is cloudy," confesses Dave Fougeron, as he ponders the next few years at Southern Star. John Nau, one of the most successful beer wholesalers in the nation, is reluctant to hazard any sort of guess in the wake of the industry upheavals of the last ten years. "I'm not going to predict," the Silver Eagle chief says. "I am going to say the consumer has now expressed a desire to have choices." Unknown is the

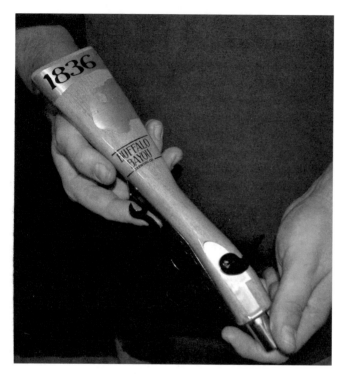

Buffalo Bayou Brewing Company became the Houston area's fifth craft brewery with the release of its 1836 copper ale, named for the year of the city's founding. *Photo by Ronnie Crocker.*

Houston beer lovers have made the annual One Pot Showdown competition, which invites teams to cook with Saint Arnold beers, a big January event. *Photo by Ronnie Crocker.*

extent to which the big breweries can fulfill those desires or how many of the small players eventually will go under or consolidate to remain competitive. Breweries have had a tough time surviving over the long haul here, but the city has changed so much that no one can say Houston is incapable of supporting a vast array of them the way far smaller cities such as Portland, San Diego or Denver do.

The near term, most people agree, looks bright. For all its millions of barrels in production, the local Bud plant has yet to make all the beer it could sell. Locally owned, locally made craft beer is rapidly building market share, and each new brewery opening adds to the awareness that all of them desperately need to grow. Wagner figures that if excitement over the newcomers expands the market by 100,000 barrels, Saint Arnold is in position to pick up its fair share of that growth.

But booms are always followed by busts, and history suggests not every beer plant in operation today will be around twenty years from now. Today's wildcatters of ale have to be bold to survive, but above all they have to make good beer. Consumers won't pay for very many duds before they return to their lower-priced mainstream beers and wonder what all the fuss was about. People who like these locally made brews need to make sure they are out there enjoying them and supporting the companies that produce them.

Houston-Area Breweries and Home-brew Clubs

BREWERIES

Get to know local brews with inexpensive brewery tours and tastings. Be aware, state law forbids you from buying beer afterward, the way you can buy a bottle of wine when visiting a winery.

Saint Arnold Brewing Company
2000 Lyons Avenue
Houston, TX 77020
Established: 1994
Signature beers: Amber, Fancy Lawnmower, Elissa IPA, Divine Reserve
  series
Tours/tastings: 3:00 p.m.–4:15 p.m. Monday–Friday, 11:00 a.m–2:00 p.m.
  Saturday, $7
Website: saintarnold.com

Southern Star Brewing Company
1207 North FM 3083 Road
Conroe, TX 77303
Established: 2008
Signature beers: Pine Belt Pale Ale, Bombshell Blonde, Buried Hatchet stout
Tours/tastings: 1:00 p.m.–3:00 p.m. Saturday, free
Website: southernstarbrewery.com

No Label Brewing Company
5373 First Street
Katy, TX 77493
Established: 2010
Signature beers: El Hefe, Ridgeback, Pale Horse Ale
Tours/tastings: 1:00 p.m.–3:00 p.m. Saturday (except first Saturday of each
    month), $5
Website: nolabelbrew.com

Karbach Brewing Company
2032 Karbach Street
Houston, TX 77092
Established: 2011
Signature beers: Weisse Versa, Sympathy for the Lager, Hopadillo IPA
Tours/tastings: 5:00 p.m.–7:00 p.m. Friday, 12:00 p.m.–3 p.m. Saturday, $7
Website: karbachbrewing.com

Buffalo Bayou Brewing Company
5301 Nolda Street
Houston, TX 77007
Established: 2012
Signature beer: 1836
Tours/tastings: A new brewery, so check website to see when tours begin
Website: buffbrew.com

Under construction:
8th Wonder Brewery
Expected opening: 2012
Website: 8thwonderbrewery.com

No longer hosting tours:
Anheuser-Busch InBev–Houston Plant
775 Gellhorn Drive
Houston, TX 77029
Established: Houston plant opened 1966; Anheuser-Busch has roots going
    back to 1852
Signature beers: Bud Light, Budweiser, ZiegenBock
Website: anheuser-busch.com

HOME-BREW CLUBS

Great resources for brewing, socializing and learning about beer. Many are based at a local home-brew shop. For example, the Foam Rangers hold their meetings and monthly brew-ins at DeFalco's Home Wine and Beer Supplies (9223 Stella Link, Houston, defalcos.com).

Bay Area Mashtronauts, Clear Lake area
mashtronauts.com

Foam Rangers, the Houston original
foamrangers.com

Kuykendahl Gran Brewers (KGB), north Houston area
thekgb.org

Brew Bayou, Clute
hbd.org/brewbayou

Cane Island Alers (CIA), Katy
cialers.com

Connoisseur's Club of Smoking and Drinking, Houston
ccsdhouston.com

Golden Triangle Homebrewers Club, Beaumont
gthcforum.proboards.com

Kingwood Homebrew Society, Kingwood
Find them on Facebook

Rogue Brewers, Humble
rogue-brewers.com

Bibliography

BOOKS

Aulbach, Louis F. *Buffalo Bayou: An Echo of Houston's Wilderness Beginnings.* Houston, TX: Louis F. Aulbach (publisher), 2012.

Buchanan, James E., ed. *Houston: A Chronological and Documentary History, 1519–1970.* Dobbs Ferry, NY: Oceana Publications, 1975.

Collected evidence and testimony from Texas Attorney General's investigation. *The Brewers and Texas Politics, Vols. I and II.* San Antonio, TX: Passing Show Printing, 1916

Fenberg, Steven. *Unprecedented Power: Jesse Jones, Capitalism, and the Common Good.* College Station: Texas A&M University Press, 2011.

Hennech, Mike. *Encyclopedia of Texas Breweries: Pre-Prohibition (1836–1918).* Irving, TX: Ale Publishing Company, 1990.

The Houston Press Club, comp. *Men of Affairs of Houston and Environs: A Newspaper Reference Work.* Houston, TX: W.H. Coyle & Company, 1913.

MacIntosh, Julie. *Dethroning the King: The Hostile Takeover of Anheuser-Busch, an American Icon.* Hoboken, NJ: John Wiley and Sons, 2011.

Okrent, Daniel. *Last Call: The Rise and Fall of Prohibition.* New York: Scribner, 2010.

One Hundred Years of Brewing: A Complete History of the Brewing Industry of the World. Chicago and New York: H.S. Rich and Company, 1903.

Pugh, Ronnie. *Ernest Tubb: The Texas Troubadour.* Durham, NC: Duke University Press, 1996.

Sandberg, Maxine Sylvia. "The Life and Career of Adolphus Busch." Master's thesis, University of Texas, Austin, 1951.

Silverthorne, Elizabeth. *Plantation Life in Texas*. College Station: Texas A&M University Press, 1986.

Stenzel, Ralph W., Jr. *The Galveston Brewery: A Galveston Landmark*. Santa Fe, TX: self-published, 1999.

Van Wieren, Dale P. *American Breweries II*. West Point, PA: East Coast Brewiana Association, 1995.

Workers of the Writers' Program of the Works Project Administration, comp. *Houston: A History and Guide*. N.p.: Works Projects Administration in the State of Texas, 1942.

Young, Dr. S.O. *A Thumb-Nail History of the City of Houston, Texas: From Its Founding in 1836 to the Year 1912*. Houston, TX: Rein & Sons Company, 1912.

NEWSPAPERS AND MAGAZINES

Advertising Age. "What a SABMiller-AB InBev Merger Would Mean in the U.S." October 6, 2011.

Dallas Morning News, accessed online via NewsBank/Readex, Database: *Historical Dallas Morning News*. Multiple publication dates.

El Domingo. El Paso, Texas. Collection of Philip Brogniez. July 15, 1923.

Galveston Daily News, accessed online via Houston Public Library and InfoTrac. Multiple publication dates.

Harby, Lee Cohen. "Texan Types and Contrasts." *Harper's Magazine*, July 1890. Accessed online via harpers.org/archive.

Houston Chronicle. Archives of the *Houston Chronicle*. Multiple publication dates.

Houston Daily Post, accessed online via U.S. Library of Congress. Multiple publication dates.

Houston Post. Archives of the *Houston Chronicle*. Multiple publication dates.

New York Times, accessed online via ProQuest Historical Newspapers: *New York Times* (1851–2007). Multiple publication dates.

Walker, Stanley. "Houston: Coolest Spot in U.S." *New York Times*, May 15, 1955. Accessed online via ProQuest Historical Newspapers.

Wall Street Journal, accessed online via ProQuest Historical Newspapers: *Wall Street Journal* (1889–1993). Multiple publication dates.

Websites, Blogs and Other Sources Accessed Exclusively Online

ab-inbev.com. "Anheusher–Busch InBev Reports Third Quarter and Nine Months 2011 Results." November 9, 2011.

Arnold v. Phillips. In re Southern Brewing Company 117 F.2d 497 (1941). Ruling of the U.S. 5th Circuit Court of Appeals. Accessed via leagle.com. February 4, 1941.

Brewers Almanac. Beer Institute. Washington, D.C., 2011. beerinstitute.org.

Brewers Association website, brewersassociation.org. Multiple locations.

DealBook blog. *New York Times.* Multiple entries. 2008. dealbook.nytimes.com.

falstaffbrewing.com/horlacher. Horlacher Brewing Company entry.

indianabeer.com. "A Brief History of Brewing in Terre Haute, Indiana."

Koch, August. Hand-drawn map of Houston in 1873. Part of the Bird's Eye Views collection of the Amon Carter Museum, Fort Worth. birdseyeviews.org.

Live Interviews

The following people were interviewed specifically for this project: Kevin Bartol, Scott Birdwell, Bev D. Blackwood II, Philip Brogniez, Dave Cohen, Dave Fougeron, Mike Heniff, John Jurgensen, Ken Knisely, Dave Maxwell, Ed Mergele, Max Miyamoto, John Nau III, Brian Royo, Susan Lieberman Seekatz, Ralph W. Stenzel Jr., Bart Truxillo, Brock Wagner and Eric Warner. Quotes from these interviews are usually attributed in the present tense. Other quotes and information in the book, including some from these same folks, are from interviews conducted over the past three years as part of the author's work for the *Houston Chronicle* and are usually attributed in the past tense.

Other

Brogniez, Philip. Unpublished history. Collection of Philip Brogniez.

Brogniez, Raymond. Unpublished history. Collection of Philip Brogniez.

The Malt Show. DVD archives. Courtesy of Bev D. Blackwood II.

Prohibition: A Film by Ken Burns and Lynn Novick. DVD. Co-production of Florentine Films and WETA. 2011.

Index

new brewery 106
production 118, 124, 125, 126
tours 114
with Silver Eagle 84, 123
Schulte, Henry 16, 17, 19
Seekatz, Susan Lieberman 54
Southern Brewing 49, 62
Southern Select 9, 36, 44, 52, 70
Southern Star 106, 121, 123, 127,
    128, 129
Spindletop 33
Stenzel, Edward 70
Stenzel, Ralph 65, 70

T

Triple XXX 43, 67, 69
Truxillo, Bart 38
Twenty-first Amendment 46

V

Village Brewery 91, 92, 94

W

Wagner, Brock 106, 107, 108, 121,
    143
Warner, Eric 131, 137, 143
Wohlfarth, Rick 83

About the Author

Ronnie Crocker is an editor and writer for the *Houston Chronicle*, where he launched the Beer, TX blog in March 2009. He was born in Galveston, grew up in the Houston area and worked as a journalist at the *Bryan–College Station Eagle* in Texas and the *Daily Press* in Newport News, Virginia, before returning home to join the *Chronicle* in 1994. He holds a bachelor's degree from Texas A&M University and a master's of business administration from the College of William and Mary. Follow his beer writing at blog.chron.com/beertx, twitter.com/rcrocker and facebook.com/rcrocker.beertx.

Photo by Patricia Shepherd.

Visit us at
www.historypress.net